DEAR PIERS MORGAN

Understanding the Implicit Connotations of your Comments on Meghan to Race

A Psychodynamic view of how we ALL ingest information, which becomes implicit.

Suzann Douglas

Dear Piers Morgan
Understanding the implicit connotations of your comments on
Meghan, to race.
By Suzann Douglas

Registered with the U.K. Copyright Service.
Registration No: 284736667

1st Edition 2020
Published by Kindle Direct Publishing
Also available in print from Kindle Direct Publishing
Contact: www.suzanndouglas.com

ISBN: 9798691513060

Dedicated to Andrew, my dear cousin, who was like a brother.

You were always so clued up on systemic inequalities.

Thanks for shining your light from 1969 - 2020

CONTENTS

FOREWORD

Written by Carl J Barge

I often tell students that counselling is a vocation like no other. After the three-year odyssey of learning about the theoretical framework, the application to self and the repeated opportunities for self-exploration, you leave the training room a different person. As a Counselling Lecturer, I can confirm the counselling training journey is an arduous one. The unknown expectations are rife, as the reasons first thought of for beginning are unconscious and will often come to fruition towards the end of the training program.

I believe this is what Suzann has achieved through writing this seminal text. As her former tutor, I can see how the course has shaped the belief in self. Through introspection, she has found an authentic voice and demonstrated that self-belief by writing a book that gets to the heart of topical issues espoused today. It is a text I will refer students to when difference and diversity seminars are scheduled.

Suzann has provided an insightful glimpse into the Internal Working Model of the human psyche, and the unconscious processes that delineate the root causes of what we are witnessing in the world. It is very much a labour of love as the passion exhibited leaps off the pages challenging the perceptions of how you see self, others and the world.

Suzann examines her own counselling training journey and subsequent challenges faced. It is through this lens that she takes the reader on an historical journey of what it means to be a person of colour within a dominant society. The associated internalised emotions that are evoked. The systemic practices at work that are at first glance unconscious, but upon closer scrutiny, we find what has been explicit all the time, draws a parallel of being "tricked, hoodwinked and bamboozled", as Malcolm X illustrated our place in the world over fifty years ago.

The treatment of Meghan Markle was the impetus for exploring what was explicit for persons of colour and implicit for those in power. The discussion of the tragic murder of George Floyd is spoken of with candour and passion. The feeling around the world has been one of shock that the breath of another human being could be extinguished for eight minutes and forty-six seconds, in the manner in which it was witnessed. As noted by Piers Morgan 'What the hell are we not seeing.'

Suzann uncovers the depth of structural racism from Africa, to the slave ships, the U.K. and America. The historical references are rich and give the reader an opportunity to weigh up what is offered, essentially asking you to decide if you will take the red pill or the blue pill in the final analysis. It has all been laid out for you to decide if what has been ingested is real and tangible.

The research undertaken is noteworthy as it supports what has been known, but ignored. Within the theoretical framework, we discuss the evidence for and the evidence against. Suzann has provided the evidence for...it is now time to decide which pill you will take.

WHY THIS BOOK

Dear Piers Morgan,

I wanted to write to you in response to your comment "Meghan and Harry haven't been criticised because of her colour but because she's a selfish social climber and he's a weak whiner - and by playing this despicable race card they have grossly libelled all of Britain". (Mail, 2020)

I felt incredibly moved by your comment, and that I should reach out to share some thoughts with you on the subject.

During writing – the horrific event occurred, where we all witnessed the horrendous killing of George Floyd on the streets of America!

Following George Floyd's despicable killing, I saw you on T.V., and there seemed to be genuine confusion from you, around how this could happen and what are some of the societal issues that foster an environment, where an event like this could occur?

You had a panel of experts on the show and seemed keen to make sense of events. You talked about the challenge "for white people to see racism, where we may not see it overtly." You questioned if "we don't have understanding, how do we affect change?" and "if that is what we are seeing on camera, what the hell are we not seeing?"

Although at the time I had already been strongly moved and had started writing, I felt motivated to complete this piece of writing.

I have been feeling moved to write for some time now. At the start of writing this book, Britain is at a boiling point of division, anger, and frustration. We are approaching the deadline for Brexit! People are frustrated; they feel distrust for politicians. There is a feeling that no-one is representing their cause, although the recent election of Boris Johnson and the conservatives seemed like an opportune moment for people to demonstrate their frustration, and the desire to "Get Brexit Done".

The far-right parties are emerging, appealing to frustrated people. The environment feels hostile and angry. Views on Brexit has separated families and communities; the pound is plummeting. People are at boiling point.

Within this environment, I have been motivated to write. Your comment above on Meghan was the final impetus that caused me to put thoughts on paper, and as I stated the killing of George Floyd was the motivation to finish writing these thoughts.

I write this book as a woman who was born and raised in the U.K. I write this book as a black woman who has experienced her entire life in the U.K. I write this book also as a counsellor, the training of which, has given me invaluable insight into my self, the human psyche and patterns of relating.

Something that prompted me to write is I noted, in the early stages of counselling training, I one day shared with my peers, as the only black person studying the course at the time, some of the difficulties I felt I was facing around race and living in the U.K. My peers seemed to listen as I offloaded the details of my experience, and also events I had encountered that day to them, (which I will share later in the chapter on 'A difficult Past').

After I had shared, one of my peers said he had a black friend that 'was always going on about things', but he thought his friend had a chip on his shoulder. He said he had never heard the emotion behind the experience before!

Therefore, I hope in sharing these thoughts, the emotion of the experience, of my living as a black woman in Britain, will be heard and not perceived as having "a chip on the shoulder"!! However, I don't want the experience captured in this writing, to be merely my own. So, to write this piece, as well as personal experiences, I have drawn on research, counselling theory and focus groups & interviews with professionals. I wanted to explore with people who have successfully built a life for themselves in the U.K., (for instance, who had made it to the position of CEO; Senior Leader, Director or Consultant, etc.,) what their perspectives would be of living as a black person within the U.K. The stories, views and the pain expressed in the focus groups, and interviews, were as I've known inherently in my experience living in the U.K. The hurt, the trauma, the impact of these experiences, were so eloquently articulated in the conversations. Many of us bear the pain and trauma of racism. I talk more in the chapter on 'trauma', how trauma does not stay contained and how 'silent, violent' histories impact us all.

Occurrences around racial repression in the U.K., are not experienced by someone calling you an offensive name, (although this does happen). Experiences of racism in the U.K. operates in a far more nuanced and covert way. It is understood and felt by those who are on the receiving end and recognised through repeated themes and occurrences. The experience is often denied by those who could never be on the receiving end, but seem to work hard to refute it and become experts about it, when it is highlighted by those who live through it. I want to talk about the process of how deeply embedded implicit bias is, how we are all recipients of ingesting the information which fosters it and how it then plays out systemically and in interactions.

It is my hope also that you will gain an understanding of the implicit connections to your comments on Meghan and race, as I explore themes and research, on how we ALL collectively ingest information, which fosters bias, and shapes our views on the world.

There are many voices out there, many voices which have remained unheard and been closed down. Thankfully, because of the horrific events we all witnessed regarding George Floyd, these voices are now being heard.

One of the most encouraging videos I watched over the last couple of days, was thousands of people kneeling outside St. Georges Hall in Liverpool, in support of the Black lives matter movement. The crowd was multicultural and also unified. It somehow restored my hope in the collective nature of us all. It re-ignited my hope that collectively, we can bring about change.

I know that talking about issues of race can be an emotive and anxiety-producing conversation. There is often strong expression, as the roots of pain go very deep. There is usually a lack of awareness for those who have never had to pay much conscious attention to issues of race.

There are lots of conversations about race taking place currently. The other day I was having a conversation with my cousin about how we move through all the issues emerging on race? I said to her that I think we must each do our bit. This book is my attempt to do my bit. I hope through this writing, you will hear and see some of the themes, that I believe, lead to a society where there is institutional racism, and we end up having a situation such as George Floyd.

INFORMATION DOWNLOAD

The Red Pill or the Blue Pill

I share the fact that I am a counsellor, as it is relevant to this writing and my current perception of the issues I will address in this book.

I am an integrative Therapist. When supporting clients, I draw on Psychodynamic theories, as well as person-centred and sometimes Cognitive Behavioral Therapy (CBT).

Whilst studying the initial stages of counselling, my peers at the time, and I, thoroughly enjoyed the learning. We were a group of about 12, and most of us had met for the 1st time on the course. We had the most incredible connection as a group! Some called it 'magical', and others referred to it as 'spiritual'. The connection we had as a group enabled us to embrace the learning together fully. The course completely changed my view of what counselling and empathy mean! Until then, I had thought empathy was sharing a similar experience that you had been through when someone was talking, showing that you understood. I learnt empathy is about really hearing, being present and understanding a person. It's about listening and seeing what they share from their perspective.

On studying the level 3 Counselling Studies, with the same group of peers, the smiling and contented faces in the room started to shift, as we began to study counselling theory and apply it to our lives. Applying the theory to our lives activated an uncomfortable shift in the way we viewed ourselves, our relationships, and our relating in the world. The work of drilling deeper had begun! We had started to tap into our implicit selves!

Beginning To Face The Rabbit Hole

On level 4 training in Therapeutic Counselling, which lasted for two academic years, and was mainly with a different and much larger group of people, the challenge intensified! I spent the first six months of the course, questioning what on earth I was doing to myself and why!? It was immensely challenging for us to apply counselling theory to self, again causing further shifts in the way we viewed ourselves, our lives and our relationships.

The challenge of the training was due to the incredible tutors that we had on the course, who constantly pushed us to apply the theory to our selves. The purpose of applying theory to self, is so that we can support clients in the room, to also push through the challenge of self-reflection, facing the discomfort of feeling difficult emotions, and journeying through to growth and change. The principle is that if a counsellor can be resilient enough to confront their difficult feelings, as opposed to avoiding them, they will be able to support a client to do the same. There was also an immense amount of course content to cover, which only intensified the challenge.

There was a temptation to carry out the study purely as an academic exercise. Still, I knew doing so would only cause the tutors to challenge my approach and push me to go back to applying the theory to myself. I wanted to quit the journey; in fact, I would say 85% of me wanted to give up! However, I then weighed up the investment I had already made, and how far I had come on the journey, and this motivated me to keep going!

The training was no longer fun! It was tough, uncomfortable, and triggering. Applying theory to self, in an emotional, congruent, non-academic way, was causing me to face parts of myself, I would have preferred to be neatly tucked away. It was an incredibly challenging journey!!

The student numbers on level 4, began to decline, as people struggled with the impact the course was having on their lives. I know I am not the only counsellor who has compared the training to the film, The Matrix, and the challenge of taking the 'red pill, or the blue pill'. "You take the blue pill - the story ends, you wake up in your bed and believe whatever you want to believe. You take the red pill - you stay in Wonderland, and I show you how deep the rabbit-hole goes" (The Matrix, 1999). I would say that to 'begin exploring the rabbit hole', or to begin facing parts of yourself which had been neatly tucked away, for a variety of reasons, was a perturbing concept.

Every time I reflected on another student that had left, I always concluded to myself, that I didn't blame anyone that quit!! We had begun to tap into our internal programming. Beginning to tap into our ingested information, posed a real challenge! It could reshape our lives; our views on our lives; ourselves, our families, our relationships, our interactions, and our beliefs.

During the training, one of the subjects that we studied was diversity. At the start of this training, some of my white counterparts were saying things, that many of us I'm sure can identify as hearing, or speaking, such as: 'I don't see race or colour'; 'I treat everyone the same', etc., etc. However, at the end of the training, some of these same peers were crying. Their awareness of issues of diversity and race had expanded. It was akin to seeing a blank template in front of you and not seeing anything, and then suddenly starting to see images and colours, emerge on the template. You suddenly begin to see something you had previously thought did not exist.

During diversity training, some of the areas we explored, were to: 'identify and explore diversity issues between [ourselves] and others. Also to 'reflect on our responses or reactions to others; to 'recognise and reflect on types of people and issues that touch our prejudices and fears'; to 'explore how a deeper understanding of diversity can enhance empathy'. (Academy, 2018). The aim of a good counsellor, as well as having empathy and care for clients, is to be self-reflective. To look honestly at how you see the world, see yourself, and to do the work on this.

Looking back, I commend my tutor's, who were able to skillfully teach such a diverse audience, from varying backgrounds and perspectives about diversity! I applaud the tutors who were so adeptly able to train on, what can be a fairly emotive subject, whilst enabling the students to be educated, engaged, respected, affirmed and challenged.

Looking back, I also value my white peers, who may not have paid much thought to issues around diversity, before studying this subject. However, they chose to allow the immersive learning experience of grasping a perspective, so different from that had been familiar to them. They embraced and journeyed through the discomfort the learning brought.

Studying the subject of diversity and the complexity of its themes, with a group of diverse students was encouraging, educational & transformational.

Throughout the course, there were issues we could have easily chosen and would have preferred to skirt over and continue with life. However, our incredible tutors continually challenged us to apply the theory to ourselves, our interactions and to drill into what was inside. To say we do not see difference is not to be honest with ourselves! It is near impossible to not notice the difference of another. You will see later in this chapter that by the age of 6 years, 18% of children, are aware of the racial stereotype of another person. Racial stereotype awareness increases to 93% by the age of 10 years. (McKown C, 2003)

I am grateful for the counselling training journey, which amongst other things, has also been key at shifting my self-concept, and enabled me to change in the way I think about issues around diversity and race. I see that we are all victims or products of the information that we have ingested, in an inequitable society. I'm aware also just how much this information influences the steering of our interactions.

I mentioned earlier; when I started writing this book, it was primarily to address your comments on Meghan Markle and to break down and highlight, how the narrative on her reporting ties into racial bias. Obviously, since then, we witnessed the appalling events of George Floyd, which I think has demonstrated the dynamic of racial oppression in its most overt and extreme form. As well as being hugely distressing and traumatic, the event has thrown up a challenge, where even the most 'blind' person to the nuances of racial oppression, have seen, there is a clear inequitable dynamic taking place. We witnessed the complete disregard for a black man and his life! The black man has already been dehumanised in the eyes of the policeman.

The killing of George Floyd has been a conversation starter, as the challenge of seeing this dynamic, causes people to question the systems that they live within. I must say I have listened to you since the killing, and I am glad to see that you are having the conversation of race on national T.V. I was grateful to hear you articulate and consider, "the rage that must build up if you are black and you are watching …and you are seeing a racist white policeman snuffing the life out of somebody, with total disregard for them, because of their skin colour". (GMB, 2020)

You seemed to have been, quite understandably, impacted from watching the video, and I could hear you repeatedly asking, "what should we now be doing?" You have asked: "whether you are black, white, what should we do to try to stop this kind of thing happening as we go forward?" You referred to the impact of watching Amy Cooper, and how she was so willing to frame a person, a black man doing nothing wrong, and that with the systemic treatment of black men in the U.S., this could have been catastrophic for this man. I heard you say on more than one occasion, "if this is what we are seeing, what are we not seeing?" (GMB, 2020)

The horrific video of George Floyd's killing seems to have challenged your thinking and opened you to hear, as it has across the world. I am glad to see there are conversations about racism now taking place, as the voices of people who have experienced this have been shunned, muted and unheard until now.

My voice is just one of many! I hope now that voices will begin to be heard.

Forming our Self Concept

Hierarchy Of Needs

When we interact in life, we do not just operate in a detached way from our inner world. On the contrary, when we interact, we function out of a wealth of information, which we have ingested over time, the majority of which remains unconscious. We ALL absorb information when growing up! This information and our responses to it then informs our choices, decisions, relationships, careers, and motivations.

Our views and our perspectives begin from the outset of our development. External figures in our world, whether that be parents, aunts or uncles, teachers, wider society, etc., act as mirrors to ourselves. We receive messages about our abilities; whether we are liked or disliked; which behaviours receive positive or negative responses; how much or how little we are responded to, and specific actions that drive those responses. We observe how adults interact with each other.

We ingest information about ourselves, about others and about the world around us. This information, and our response to these messages, leads to us forming conclusions about ourselves and others. We are developing our 'self-concept', that is: forming what we believe about, and how we perceive ourselves, as well as our concept of others. We are all participants and recipients of this process.

You may be familiar with the Hierarchy of Needs (Abraham Maslow), which greatly influenced the development of Carl Rogers Person-Centred Therapy. The premise is that each person born on this earth has basic needs. These needs are **Physiological**: for food, water, shelter, rest, warmth, etc.; **Safety**: for emotional security, stability, physical safety, etc.; **Love / Belonging**: for intimate relationships, family and friends, trust, being part of a group, acceptance, etc.; **Esteem**: prestige and feeling of accomplishment, etc.; **Self-actualisation**: achieving one's full potential, including creative activities.

In an ideal world, a person would have the first level of needs met, and be satisfied, and then progress on to the 2nd level and so forth and so forth.

I am sure you can imagine, for many people, along the process of growth, some of these needs are not satisfied, for a variety of reasons. Carl Rodgers, the founder of Person-Centred Therapy, believed that once a person had overcome any barriers to having these needs met, they could then reach the place of Self-Actualisation, that is: being the best version of themselves they could be.

There is a handy chart below from Simply Psychology. In their diagram, they have labelled the 1st four needs as deficiency needs. "Deficiency needs arise due to deprivation and are said to motivate people when they are unmet. Also, the motivation to fulfil such needs will become stronger the longer the duration they are denied. For example, the longer a person goes without food, the more hungry they will become." (Psychology, 2020)

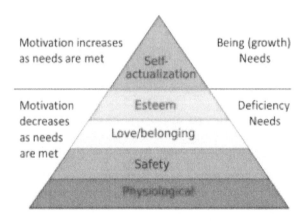

So, we are all born into this world, with basic needs, and in an ideal world, these needs, physiological, psychological and emotional, are healthily met. Obviously, in our formative years, we are unable to meet these needs by ourselves. As mentioned previously, the adults in our world begin to operate as 'mirror's' to ourselves, and we start to learn about 'who they think we are', from the interactions we have with them.

Lots of counselling theories and models talk about this process in different ways. There are a vast range of theories which Counsellors and Psychotherapists use to inform their work. In this section, I will explore just 2 of a whole range of theories, but the premise remains the same, all people are born with needs, and require these needs to be healthily met.

Attachment Theory

Attachment Theory – (Bowlby J / Ainsworth M). This fascinating theory explores how a mother attaches to her child, and the impact the attachment style then has on a person's interactions in life. Accompanying this theory, is a whole table of projections, on the outcomes on the personality you are likely to have, according to your attachment style. When I initially looked at this table, I totally rejected the theory! I always had the notion that I was someone who made their own choices in life. I felt I was "not going to be determined by a projection on a table – thank you very much"!

However, it was hugely humbling and impactful when I began to realise that I had been the typical outcome of my attachment style to my mother. I had to work and grow through this information, and it gave me insight and impetus to change.

So, based on a child's relationship with their mother, there are a range of possible ways this affects a person relating in the world. For example, the attachment style may have been '**Secure**' - resulting in a person naturally feeling confident and having faith in their abilities. A person with a secure attachment exposure would more likely end up being resilient and independent. Or a person may have experienced an '**Avoidant**' attachment style, where the mother was dismissive, critical, irritable, distant, etc. A person who had this type of attachment style may feel rejected or isolated in life. They may also tend to feel stressed and scared. There is also an '**Ambivalent**' attachment style, where a mother may have been inconsistent, indifferent and insensitive. A person who experienced this type of attachment may feel stressed and insecure, angry and susceptible to feeling emotional abandonment. They may be unsociable and aggressive. Or there is the '**Disorganised**' attachment style, where a mother may have been unpredictable or inspired fear. She may have been an addict or experienced a mental disorder. This type of exposure could lead to a person feeling scared and sad, with low self-esteem. They may also feel angry and be passive.

There is a handy diagram below, which simplifies attachment theory and the anticipated outcomes on a person.

(Upbility, 2020)

Digging a little deeper into this theory, Bowlby believed that in addition to the attachment style between caregiver and child, the child also builds an internal template of self, called the 'Internal Working Model'. "In the working model of the world that anyone builds a key feature is his notion of who his attachment figures are, where they may be found, and how they may be expected to respond. Similarly, in the working model of the self that anyone builds a key feature is his notion of how acceptable or unacceptable he himself is in the eyes of his attachment figures." (Bowlby, 1973)

This internal working model is continually built by a person, from the cradle to the grave, and forms an inner framework of how a person feels about themselves, e.g., secure, loved, worthy, unworthy, etc. This internal template also sets expectations a person has on relationships and acts as the filter through which one perceives interactions.

So, you can imagine, already in just exploring one theory and looking at interactions, if you take the typical workplace, for example, you will have people with a range of attachment styles. There might be those interacting out of confidence and independence; some may tend to feel rejected or isolated, even in a crowd. Some may tend to be stressed, insecure and angry, and there might be those with low self-esteem. This influence of attachment in interaction styles is without even looking into the day to day personal factors of life, that affect us all and adding in the additional element of social and racial perspective, relative for this book.

The theory of attachment was one I wanted to include in this book, as I believe it has such powerful implications on us all. I do not believe in being fatalistic and think the implications need not be permanent. I feel insight into our attachment styles, can bring us understanding and support some of the ways we may want to shift if any. Having positive relationships in adult life, as well as healing (including talking therapies) can also help to settle and balance out attachment issues.

In doing the focus groups and interviews on Implicit Bias, attachment for BAME people was an issue that came up. This is due to the huge cost paid by our communities, in responding to calls to come and work in the U.K.

"After the Second World War, 1939 – 1945, Britain was in need of labour in order to aid the process of rebuilding the country which had been severely devastated in some areas, particularly London and the industrial cities. 'Subjects' from the Caribbean colonies were called upon to help 'the mother country', and people with a strong reverence for England responded to the call and came to help" (Arnold; Opoku, 2020). "Between 1955 and 1960 adults leaving the Caribbean for the United Kingdom, Canada and the USA took with them 6,500 children and left behind 90,000." (Thomas, 2014)

Over the years, I have met many people who have experienced this type of upbringing, where children were left with grandparents, separated from siblings, in order for their parents to support the rebuilding of the U.K. Sometimes the older sibling had to look after the younger ones, never really having the right to be a child, having a tremendous amount of responsibility on their shoulders. I have heard the stories of the impact on family relationships, including not bonding, abandonment and resentment. I have heard the story of someone who was so overloaded in trying to be this responsible person as a child, well ahead of her time, that she ended up having a breakdown.

When a person experiences broken mirroring from the external world, it can lead to trauma. "Any style of attachment — other than secure attachment — can lead to trauma. The ability to regulate one's emotions isn't built-in. It's taught in one's earliest relationships, ingrained throughout childhood, and practised throughout life. What is emotional regulation? It's the ability to ride the waves of life's ups and downs, to deal with change, and create a safe space to share emotions in healthy relationships." (LLP, 2018)

Undealt with trauma does not just disappear, and it can rarely be contained. Trauma will find a way of expression. Undealt with trauma also travels down the generations (intergenerationally) and has the ability to cause epigenetic changes.

There are some fascinating areas of study, that look at the impact the past plays, in quite literally re-shaping the present of an individual, such as medical anthropology. In this area of study, we learn how "intergenerational effects and environmental exposures become embodied in an individual's lifespan, and may cause intergenerational effects by epigenetic changes, amongst others. Our bodies are historical processes and historical sites." (Theidon, 2020)

Later in this book, in the section on trauma, I will explore how research shows, that due to the history of slavery, the avoidant and ambivalent attachment styles have affected many people intergenerationally. This effect has been on both the descendants of slaves and the descendants of slave owners.

Ego Distortion

Another theory I thought important to include is Winnicott's theory of true self and false self. In his theory, he explores how in our early relationships (his focus is particularly on the mother), we learn whether our true selves are responded to and accepted. He talks about our gestures as infants, "that gives expression to a spontaneous impulse; the source of the gesture is the True Self." (Winnicott, 2018) It is how these gestures, which are expressions of the true self, are responded to, that causes us to develop and build our real personality. However, if there is a lack of acceptance for our true selves, we then learn to be "like mother, nurse, aunt, brother, or whoever at the time dominates the scene." (Winnicott, 2018) In compliance, we then operate out of that False Self in the world, although there are varying degrees to which we can do this.

Within his theory of True Self and False Self, Winnicott also explores Ego Distortion, where he develops on I.D. and Ego. You may be familiar with I.D. and Ego from Freud's model of the psyche. I.D. being the part of our primal instincts, Superego being the moralistic parts of ourselves and what we think we 'should' or 'should not' be doing; and ego being the regulator of both I.D. and Superego.

In Winnicott's theory, he expands that for an infant, I.D. instincts are not yet internalised, that is clearly defined as internal to the infant. These "instincts can be as much external as can a clap of thunder or a hit." (Winnicott, 2018)

In an ideal world, through healthy mirroring, a person learns to integrate these instincts. When there is not a healthy development, those parts of ourselves can get almost frozen in time, although we expand around those parts. We can go on to build careers, marry, parent, become grandparents, while those parts of ourselves have not been afforded healthy development.

The following is what I believe to be an example of ego distortion, although I would say trauma certainly was a factor in these events. The following demonstrates how the information we have ingested, can leak into our interactions with the world, our relationships, etc. This is a fusion of real observed events, which emerged at a time when I was studying and starting to apply theory to my life and understand things through the lens of theory. The names and some details have been changed to protect the identity of the individuals.

Mary and Tom

Mary recently remarried. She had previously been in an abusive marriage. She met Tom, they both fell in love, and he then joined her in the U.K.

Mary spent much of her time volunteering in a community charity. In this charity, some of the roles were paid, and some were unpaid. Her husband was highly qualified and accredited for one of the senior charity roles in his home country. However, in the U.K. his credentials were not recognised, meaning he would need to retrain for a further five years, to qualify for undertaking the senior role on a paid basis. Tom then began to volunteer with Mary. Mary and Tom obviously needed an income and were impacted by not having or securing paid work.

Mary had experienced sexual abuse when she was growing up, which means her need for safety was violated (pyramid of needs). This also means the powerful element of trauma may have been present.

After many years of service, the existing senior lead of the charity decided to move on. Possibly, Mary and Tom hoped this was a time where Tom could start earning a living, as the senior leader in the charity. However, unfortunately, the doors remained closed, and the frustration and anger of this, triggered a whole series of events, for Mary.

Mary then began to post multiple messages a day on Facebook, attacking the charity, their staff and their ethos. This went on for a long while. Mary then lodged an allegation of assault, to the charities trust about the ex-senior lead, involving another member of the charity. The allegation meant the trust then had to investigate this complaint, which led to reputational damage of the ex-senior leader. The charity was destabilised, as not only were they left to operate without a senior leader, they now had to process through and deal with the allegations, which when investigated emerged as being unfounded.

When observing all of this, I felt that – this was really about Mary's undealt with trauma! I felt that Mary was now in a new relationship, in which she felt safe, and the trauma that she had been unable to face was surfacing. The situation felt so explosive at the time; I did not feel it was safe to approach Mary about her trauma.

I also reflected on the theory of instincts becoming internalised. If a person's development becomes stunted at the point where "instincts can be as much external as can a clap of thunder or a hit", then life could be a reactive experience. For example, if you have **Physiological needs** for shelter, rest & warmth, and also **Safety needs** for emotional security, stability and physical safety, and those have been unmet or violated, you would not have completed the process of integrating those needs. It could mean on an unconscious level, for instance: when you are volunteering for a charity that is meant to help people, you might be thinking or feeling 'where is my help?' You may be wounded at a primal level and interpret them closing the door to employing your husband, as them closing the door on, or not helping you.

Mary has since calmed down, and she has got some therapy. She is now talking about the trauma she realises she is carrying and its impact. Her posts are now all about trauma and its effects on body and mind.

Forming our Concept of 'The Other'

Racial And Social Perspective Theory

Before I talk about forming our racial and social perspectives, research shows scholars view race, not as an actual, but as a social construct, created by dominant groups. Following the emergence of the Atlantic slave trade, there was the "further incentive to categorise human groups in order to justify the subordination of African slaves." (Meltzer, 1993) At this time Europeans began to sort themselves and 'others' into groups based on physical appearance. Links were then made between physical differences and embedded beliefs about the "inherited intellectual, behavioral, and moral qualities." (Banton, 1977)

According to the American Anthropological Association, "Evidence from the analysis of genetics (e.g., DNA) indicates that most physical variation, about 94%, lies within so-called racial groups. Conventional geographic 'racial' groupings differ from one another only in about 6% of their genes. This means that there is greater variation within 'racial' groups than between them... Throughout history whenever different groups have come into contact, they have interbred. The continued sharing of genetic materials has maintained all of humankind as a single species." (Association, 1998) Yet we have fostered such strong identities and associations to 'race' based on colour.

The school curriculum is an instrumental part of how we form our concept of 'the other.' The curriculum strongly influences the history that is taught, (which is explored in the chapter on 'A Difficult Past'). The curriculum also affects press reporting, (which is expanded on in the chapter on 'The Press, The Messages Continue').

As children, when growing, in addition to ingesting information about ourselves, we are continually intaking information about others. As previously stated, we view how adults around us interact with other people. We consider the responses of the people with whom they interact. We gather messages about both the adults around us, and we gather assumptions about the people with whom they communicate. We also listen to the messages we are taught about 'the other', which informs our concept. For instance, a simplistic and familiar example, when I was growing up, cowboy and Indian films were hugely popular. I am sure we can all agree, we knew who the inferred 'heroes' were in the movies and who the 'villains' were. There has obviously been much debate over the years about these movies.

These cowboy and Indian identities would be re-enacted in play, and of course, everyone wanted to be the 'heroes'. Even in this example, we have a simple, but powerful narrative which is being embedded into the minds of society. These films were part of the culture when I was growing up, and a cowboy and Indian film would be on T.V. most weeks. "Yet this popularity has not always been matched...[in] academic circles. With a few exceptions..., Western fiction has usually been relegated to the sphere of popular culture and has been criticised for its perceived use of stereotyped and shallow characters, basic plotlines, predictable outcome and uncreative use of language (Wallman x-xi; Cawelti 3-9). Yet American Western fiction has not only shaped American culture and society but also the way Americans perceive America." (Fernández, 2009)

Popular British culture has certainly also been influenced by American fiction. Many of us have gone to the cinema excited to see the latest Hollywood Blockbuster. I have some family members who are heavily into the Avengers movie franchise and follow every plot and character! I am not a huge fan, but one day decided to go and watch Avengers: Infinity War with them. However, I remember being really engaged with the movie and totally flabbergasted at the end, when most of the main characters died.

The cinema audience was in silence, and we all sat there through the credits, seemingly questioning, this can't be how this ends! However, the credits scrolled right to the end, and there was no sign of the characters coming back to life. The audience, including myself, seemed to leave the cinema quietly stunned. When Endgame, the sequel film came out, I had to go and see it to get closure and answers on the preceding movie.

Such is the power of cinema, or literature, or media per se. My family members set up an avenger's chat group. There were plans to watch some of the movies together. There were conversations about the plot and predictions about what would happen. It was a bonding experience; it was a stirring experience.

There has been exploration about the concept of the 'Americanization' of Britain through films and seeking to understand its dominance, whether this is because of culture or the struggle of the British film industry. Mark Glancy (film historian) counters this with what he calls the 'hidden history' revealed in 2005, where "the British Film Institute published its ranking of 'the U.K.'s 100 most popular films.' Based on a tally of tickets sold...stretching back to include...every decade since the 1930s." (Glancy, 2014) There were some surprises with the most successful British film being Spring in Park Lane (1948) and the U.S. Gone with the wind in 1st place.

Films have a huge influence on culture. Films draw us in; they entertain, they inform, they stimulate, they educate. There is often the question of whether life imitates art or vice versa. Sometimes there are items on the news agenda, which you think if you had seen in a movie, would not have been believed —for instance, considering COVID-19, who would have imagined a time where we would all be facing lockdown and staying at home.

Films impact culture and culture impacts film. There is much debate about what draws us (and such huge audiences) into a movie. One writer explores the element of the "pleasure principle structuring spectator identification..." (Everett, 1995-1996) The pleasure principle is a Freudian concept of "the instinctive seeking of pleasure and avoiding of pain to satisfy biological and psychological needs." (C.R. Snyder, 2006)

In terms of looking at how films and media help to inform our social and racial perspectives, as much as the clever plots that draw audiences in and keep them enticed, there is, as with many industries, a huge lack of diversity in the film industry and its decision-makers.

The Washington Post explored "The staggering numbers that prove Hollywood has a serious race problem... Academy of Motion Picture Arts and Sciences directors branch [who help decide Oscar nominees are] 89 per cent male and 84 percent white, and roughly half are 60 or older, a Washington Post analysis found." (Post, 2016)

An infographic in 2015, which illustrated the diversity gap in the Academy Awards over its history 1927 to 2015 highlighted that:

- 99% of Best Actress winners have been white
- 92% of Best Actor winners have been white

- 93% of Academy voters are white and 76% are male
- 99% of Best Director winners have been male

(ADL, 2020)

How does this lack of diversity influence film and the content that is created, which in turn has a huge influence on culture? "The significance of film in American culture inheres in its ability both to reflect and interpret society. Individual works of cinema, treating historical, social, or fictional topics, emanate from the director's perception of events. Moreover, these insights are shaped by the filmmaker's *Weltanschauung* [philosophy or view of life], which is then translated and refined on screen." (Sanders, 1984)

In 2016 many members of the film community boycotted the Oscars, including Will Smith, due to lack of diversity. I guess, therefore encouraging diversity naturally creates a broader lens for us all.

In terms of forming our social and racial perspectives, a dynamic we ingest, which often goes undetected and under the radar is the concept of 'the norm and the other', reflected across culture, including in press reporting and media. For instance, only 'the other' is identified by race or religion. This is a theme that is common in news and media, which is influenced by the school curriculum. The challenge with the social construct of race is that 'White' becomes the unseen, the norm, the template and all that can be seen is 'the other'.

Professor Alistair Bonnett (British sociologist) "observes that 'Whiteness is a centred identity. In other words, Whiteness has, at least within the modern era and within Western Societies, tended to be constructed as a norm, an unchanging and unproblematic location, a position from which all other identities come to be marked by their difference'". (Ann Blake, 2001)

This identity of white as the norm and anything else as 'the other' becomes so embedded in psyche and implicit, that it's almost invisible. I talk more about this implicit and imperceptible nature of white as the norm later in this book, in exploring the reaction and offence to John Snow referring to people as 'white' in a news report.

Children are constantly observing interactions and therefore learning about the world around them. They are learning about values given to themselves and others. "When children come to understand that others endorse stereotypic beliefs, they gain an insight into others' social motives that profoundly affects their relationship to other individuals, social settings, and society. Awareness that others endorse stereo- types--...referred to as stereotype consciousness, represents a radical change in children's understanding of the social world, and its consequences are not hard to imagine" (Clark McKown, 2003)

The research on 'stereotype consciousness', also talks about 'stereotype threat.' For instance, a child aware of the stereotype projected onto them might be aware they will be judged through this stereotype when taking a test. Their performance therefore, might be impacted by the expectation and judgement. "Since its introduction into the academic literature, stereotype threat has become one of the most widely studied topics in the field of social psychology." (T Schmader, 2008) "Stereotype threat has been argued to show a reduction in the performance of individuals who belong to negatively stereotyped groups." (C.M. Steel, 1964)

I know how expectations projected onto you have the potential to affect results, if you allow. For instance, I once had a boss, and (I believe probably because of the messages he had ingested when growing up) his whole focus was on mistakes. He was a nice person, not much of an encourager; however, if there ever was a mistake, this is where he became very powerfully communicative. He could not tolerate mistakes. He focused on mistakes. He escalated mistakes!

However, this did not foster a productive team atmosphere, and the team became demotivated, demoralised and on edge. We all make mistakes, but I found that when working for him, I would at times, make mistakes I had never made in my life. I remember one particular mistake, thinking, of *all* the people to make that mistake with, I did it with him. I knew that he would be enraged. It's almost as if his expectation of mistakes literally drew them out of the entire team and me.

Children are continually intaking messages about the world around them. "All identity is cultural and begins early. Racial awareness-that is, a sense of one's own racial identity and that of others, as well as awareness of racial difference, begins in the first few years of life." (Naughton, 2006) A study shows that by the age of 6 years, 18% of children can deduce another individuals stereotype. By the age of 10 years 93% "of children are able to infer an individual's stereotype." (Clark McKown, 2003) A separate study "Goodman (1964) defined three stages in the development of racial attitude: 1. Racial awareness (from age 2), in which a child learns to perceive and label racial differences; 2. Racial orientation (age 3-6), in which the first positive and negative evaluation is apparent; 3. Racial attitudes (age 6-8), in which there is a gradual intensification of in-group and out-group preferences and prejudices." (Naughton, 2006)

Research shows how derogatory descriptions of 'the other' were used to construct the hierarchy of race, which then became embedded as beliefs.

There are many avenues that support in helping us to adopt social and racial perspectives, which then become embedded and implicit. In her book White Fragility, Robin DiAgelo writes that "we are socialised into these groups collectively. In mainstream culture, we all receive the same messages about what these groups mean, why being in one group is a different experience from being in another. And we also know that it is 'better' to be in one of these groups than to be in its opposite.... We gain our understanding of group meaning collectively through aspects of the society around us that are shared and unavoidable: television, movies, news items, song lyrics, magazines, textbooks, schools, religion, literature, stories, jokes, traditions and practices, history and so on." (DiAngelo, 2019)

We can see that just by living and operating in the way we are, we are passing on messages about race to the generations below us. I guess we all need to consider, do we really want to continue to foster a world where another George Floyd event can happen in this generation, or in generations to come?

In the next chapter, we can look at how this information we have ingested becomes implicit, and some of the ways we then begin to operate out of it.

THE POWER OF THE UNCONSCIOUS

We Suppress Information Ingested

L et's face it, no human being wants to run towards pain; it is counterintuitive!! We run away from pain. We want to feel good emotions! If there is difficult stuff, we often find ways to keep ourselves elevated above feeling it, whether that be through busyness, work, food, alcohol, whatever the avoidance method is. Most of us only end up in the counselling room or exploring what might be taking place, when our ways of operating are proving to be problematic. Situations of pain and discomfort, trigger introspection, and these times afford us the opportunity to do some internal work.

We can then begin to explore, how have I reached this point; what is going on for me; how did I get here? Within the light of exploration, we can begin to gain awareness of the things that are going on beyond our consciousness.

For instance, a few years ago, I was carrying out my usual 'busy' routine, and then noticed a patch of grey over my eyesight. It was strange! I decided to monitor it, but it started to get worse, so I went to Moorfield's Eye Hospital, A&E department. They told me it was optic neuritis, and started doing further tests to investigate what might be going on behind it.

I carried on as usual and was still travelling to and from work, and then one day decided to pop into my Drs surgery, as I had a bit of pain on top of it all. When I reeled off to my Dr, I had optic neuritis and had come to see her about pain, she repeated, "optic neuritis?" My Dr seemed to be alarmed that I had the condition, and was still carrying on as normal, and said, "I think it's OK for you not to work at the moment!". My Dr advised me to slow down and rest. I promptly followed her advice.

I then went back to Moorfield's for the results of the tests, and to my shock was told that they thought it was indicative of Multiple Sclerosis!! It took ages for the news to sink in! However, at the time, I knew there was a specific ongoing situation in my life that I was finding incredibly stressful. On getting that news, it was a wake-up call!! I made a complete overhaul in my life, removing the stress. I didn't want the prognosis to escalate. Thankfully, with the overhaul, things have been stable and not escalated since that time. My eyesight has returned to normal, and I have never been diagnosed with the condition.

From my life experience, from my training as a counsellor, and exposure to the book during training, 'the body keeps the score' (Van-Der-Kolk, 2014), it's led me to the work of Dr Gabor Maté (Physician). In his talks, Dr Maté often explores the connection with stress and disease.

So, we generally don't explore things, until our ways of operating become unhelpful or give us unsatisfactory results. The situation with George Floyd has caused a worldwide global movement, where people can see that systemically things are not working, and they are now ready to start exploring in different ways, how we have got to this place.

We've explored in the previous chapter, that by the age of 10, a child has already absorbed formative information, in terms of race and class. They have also absorbed messages about themselves. Some of these messages may be positive on the psyche; some of these may be negative. A child will already be aware of his or her social standing in the world and how they are regarded. They would have already been through their particular style of attachment, which has influenced their expectations in life and interactions. There is a myriad of possibilities that each individual may have experienced.

Because all this information, however, the 'good' and the 'bad', is too overwhelming to hold, most of it becomes subconscious and therefore not accessible to us consciously. It takes self-reflection and exploration to even begin to tap into or access some of it.

We are left with our 'field of awareness' (Firman F, 1997), that is the parts of us that we *can* see, or are *consciously* aware of. Within this part of us that stays conscious, we operate out of our "stable and adjusted existence. We are protected from Pain & Perfection or Trauma & Idealisation. We operate with our Survival Personalities or false Self. Using our Defence Mechanisms or Addictions." (Firman F, 1997)

This is certainly not the end of the story! In a safe way, we can certainly begin to access more parts of ourselves, whether that be through therapy, self-reflection, healing, faith, etc.. In accessing more parts of ourselves, it means the amazing memories that are unconscious will come up, as well as the not so pleasant memories. Even if one may not have had affirming external mirroring relationships when growing up, this can be built into life. Having loving, supportive relationships around us, supports growth.

Some of the Ways we Operate out of the Unconscious

Professionals – With Addictions

Whilst studying, I really enjoyed learning about the work of Firman & Gila, and their book 'The Primal Wound'. The book begins with their Addiction/ Abuse workshop for professionals. It looks at their study on why these professionals, would choose these addictions despite the harmful effects, even though they sometimes posed a danger to life.

Addictions can manifest in many forms, workaholism, overeating, alcohol, drugs, sex, etc. The professionals they worked with were experiencing addictions in:

- Alcohol
- Drugs
- Sex
- Food
- Obsessive relationships with lovers/ spouses/ children
- Compulsivity in personal and professional lives

They asked participants "to imagine themselves in a situation during which they were beginning to feel the urge to engage in their addiction. They were encouraged to allow themselves to feel this urge as much as they possibly could, but then to imagine they chose not to perform the addictive behaviour. Instead of acting out the addiction, they simply sat with this pressing urge as it cried out for expression…They were asked to get to the very bottom of it…to the absolute core." (Firman F, 1997) Participants were asked to share what they found.

The following are a list of feelings that emerged behind the addictions.

- Disintegration
- Worthlessness
- Lost
- Disconnection
- Lack of existence
- Invisible
- Bad
- Evil
- Void
- Vacuum
- Abandoned
- Alone
- Powerless
- Wimpy
- Wrong
- Tense
- Paranoid
- Not breathing, nonbeing
- Humiliated
- Shame
- Unloved

The feelings these participants felt, were so uncomfortable that they were unconsciously trying to avoid them. They were choosing addictions that were in many cases damaging and at times, a threat to life, to avoid the pain they were feeling.

So, we have an example of people who have been through the early experiences of not having a healthy facilitating mirror. In their book, Firman and Gila refer to this as non-being, which creates a primal wound.

This group of people were trying to survive in the world, being fueled by their early experiences, and used addictions, to escape what they were feeling and numb the pain.

Addiction is one manifestation, of operating out of implicit pain and attempting to avoid it. We are all navigating the complexity of living out of absorbed information.

There has been much debate over the years about the causes of addictions, whether these are caused by genetic factors, neurological disorders, brain chemistry, self-esteem, etc. There have been tests performed with rats, namely 'Rat Park' in the 1970s to see whether rats would become addicted to morphine. The rats were divided into four test groups, held in either isolated cages, or 'Rat Park', which was a much larger environment with food, things for the rats to play with and space to mate.

In both environments were two bottles, one containing sweetened morphine and the other plain tap water. Notably, the rats in the caged environment were drawn to drinking morphine, but the rats in the larger environment with more amenities preferred the tap water.

There were debates about what that initial and further tests concluded, although some believed it showed that "environmental enrichment...may provide protection against the development of drug addiction." (Marcello Solinas, 2008)

Obviously, anyone wanting help for addiction should seek professional and experienced support. Even in looking at guidance from those with long-established records of counselling those with addictions it says: "Substance abuse treatment involves talking about and expressing intense and possibly painful emotions such as guilt, resentment, anger and despair...Additionally it also involves recalling frightening or challenging parts of a person's personal history, such as maltreatment and trauma." (Faulkner, 2019)

In one of his Ted Talks, Dr Gabor Maté, who has worked with many people with addictions, says that "what addicts get is a release from pain...a sense of peace, a sense of control, a sense of calmness, very, very temporarily." (Mate, 2015) He then goes on to say that drugs like heroin, morphine, codeine, cocaine, alcohol, are all pain killers.

Dr Maté then goes on to talk about an interesting dynamic of him being born to Jewish parents in Budapest Hungary. He was two months old when the German occupation moved in, and his mother apparently called the paediatrician, as he was crying all the time. However, on calling the paediatrician told her, 'all my Jewish babies are crying'.

He talks about babies "picking up on the stresses and the terrors and the depression of our mothers"... (Mate, 2015). He talks about passing on "the trauma and the suffering unconsciously from one generation to the next." (Mate, 2015) He also talks about how this sense of 'not being wanted, because my mother isn't happy around me', caused him to feel an emptiness, which he then filled with his own addictions to work and obsession with classical music.

Although there are debates about the causes of addictions, from life experience, the themes above resonate with me. As mentioned previously, in researching for this book, the element of trauma, resounding through the generations, was a repeated theme which kept on emerging.

Defence Mechanisms

Exploring Amy Cooper
So, how do we get to a world, where there are such explosive situations, like Amy Cooper? How do we arrive at a place, where an innocent bird watcher, who is Harvard educated, can be walking in the park, and encounter a woman, so furious at him asking her to put her dog on a leash, that she operates in that way. Amy is so enraged, she drags the poor dog with her, in such a way, that his front legs cannot even touch the floor. She then ensues to call the cops and tell them that an African American man is provoking her in a park? As we know, the situation could have been catastrophic for a black male, having a white woman call the police about him.

In the video, Amy says: "I'm going to tell them there is an African American man, threatening my life." The effortlessness at which Amy reached for her phone and was prepared to frame the black man in front of her, with no regard for the consequences, which could have been disastrous for him, is incredible! Regardless of whether Amy chooses to admit it consciously, or not, she was clearly aware of the systemic racially-biased structures she lives within. By her very actions, Amy knew that as a white woman, she would be systemically regarded and protected. Amy instinctively knew that Christian, the black male, would not be regarded, possibly not believed, and not heard. In her rage and anger, Amy uses her awareness of this dynamic to hurt Christian, the black male, and to attack him.

Amy has implicitly learnt that within and by society, she is granted, respected, regarded and given more privilege than black males are. In her rage, Amy, therefore, lashes out to hurt Christian, the black male. Amy immediately knew that socially, with her privilege, Christian was in the weaker position. In her anger, or in response to whatever was taking place for her, she attacked him and displaced her emotions onto him.

You can see how instinctive these responses were, at the moment that she operated, sitting out of sight and out of consciousness. This is a demonstration of the implicit in operation, and why it takes becoming self-aware and adopting some honesty, to even tap into our motivations. This is also a demonstration of why the counselling training became so uncomfortable, as we all began to tap into and to see our drivers and motivations, in respective areas of life.

In her paper on Undoing Racism and Understanding White Privilege, Dr Francis e Kendall Writes: "We are able to grow up without our racial supremacy's being questioned. It is so taken for granted, such a foundation of all that we know, that we are able to be unconscious of it even though it permeates every aspect of our lives. Charles W. Mills describes this phenomenon in his book The Racial Contract (Ithaca: Cornell University Press, 1997). '...white misunderstanding, misrepresentation, evasion, and self-deception on matters related to race are...psychically required for conquest, colonisation, and enslavement. And these phenomena are in no way accidental, but prescribed by the terms of the Racial Contract, which requires a certain schedule of structured blindness and opacities in order to establish and maintain the white polity.' (p. 19, italics his)." (Kendall, 2002)

The alarming thing is that, at the time, Amy was a senior employee of a financial services institution. Whilst carrying out the focus groups and interviews to discuss how implicit bias manifests in our systems, I interviewed a BAME American professional. She said to me, "let's face it, the probability that I might be shot or accosted by the police is very low, very slim. However, the probability that I will encounter an Amy Cooper, that makes decisions about my career, is very high!" This woman is currently facing an arduous battle to be promoted further, so familiar to BAME people.

Dr Kendall writes: "We who are white can be absolute jerks and still have white privileges; people of color can be the most wonderful individuals in the world and not have them". (Kendall, 2002)

Imagine this dynamic and interplay of privilege with access to influence and power, versus the stigmatised, racialised, repressed and restricted from access to power, playing out in institutions all across the U.K. and U.S.

I will explore more about the outworking of bias and how it manifests in our systems, later. For now, I want to continue the journey on how we operate out of ingested information.

Whilst I do not know Amy, have not researched about her, and do not purport to speak about her personal case, I am observing her interaction in the park, through the lens of counselling theory perspective. The beautiful thing about counselling is it is bespoke, and different minds will have different views or insights. In counselling, we work collaboratively, in that the British Association of Counselling and Psychotherapy (BACP) has a requirement that all counsellors work under supervision. Supervision is used to support, steer, and develop clinical practice, and it is all established around the safety of the client. Working with a supervisor or in a peer group is an excellent experience as you gain access to other minds and perspectives, to support practice.

It has taken many minds to shape and define many models, which counsellors of today can use to support their work, and I am sure future therapist will continue to define and create. We work collaboratively, always supported by research, peers, supervision and drawing on opinions.

So, shifting slightly away from the embedded implicit bias, that is mixed into the cocktail of our generic ways of growth, let's look at defence mechanisms. Using defence mechanisms – are one of the ways that we subconsciously choose to operate, to manage and avoid feeling uncomfortable stimuli. Some of these defence mechanisms may be denial (choosing to ignore information which is too difficult to accept); reaction formation (voicing in the most extreme way, the exact opposite of what you really feel because those feelings cause anxiety); projection (placing feelings about oneself, that are too uncomfortable to face, onto another). The list goes on and on.

There are many defence mechanisms. There is a lovely table from simply psychology, which I have included overleaf, which shows six types of defence mechanisms and how they might play out, in a way that is easy to understand.

Mechanism	Description	Example
Repression	Repression is an unconscious mechanism employed by the ego to keep disturbing or threatening thoughts from becoming conscious.	During the Oedipus complex aggressive thoughts about the same sex parents are repressed
Denial	Denial involves blocking external events from awareness. If some situation is just too much to handle, the person just refuses to experience it.	For example, smokers may refuse to admit to themselves that smoking is bad for their health.
Projection	This involves individuals attributing their own unacceptable thoughts, feeling and motives to another person.	You might hate someone, but your superego tells you that such hatred is unacceptable. You can 'solve' the problem by believing that they hate you.
Displacement	Satisfying an impulse (e.g. aggression) with a substitute object.	Someone who is frustrated by his or her boss at work may go home and kick the dog.
Regression	This is a movement back in psychological time when one is faced with stress.	A child may begin to suck their thumb again or wet the bed when they need to spend some time in the hospital.
Sublimation	Satisfying an impulse (e.g. aggression) with a substitute object. In a socially acceptable way.	Sport is an example of putting our emotions (e.g. aggression) into something constructive.

(Psychology, 2019)

I do not know Amy Cooper, but perceive on the recording, she seemed in a hugely reactive and angry place. Perhaps she was feeling one of the emotions listed in the Firman and Gila table, which the professionals in the Addiction and Abuse workshop had expressed, when accessing what it is that they were *really* feeling, underneath their behaviours?

It seems there was a case of displacement and Projection taking place. Perhaps, in this case, there was possibly something going on for Amy in the area of relationship (be it family, romantic or otherwise)? Her emotional pain was being triggered, and she was responding angrily. She seemed in a place of rage. Her poor dog was not even able to put his feet on the ground and was being dragged around. Whatever experience had been triggered for Amy Cooper and had been tapped into, it was manifesting in rage and being displaced and projected out onto Christian.

Amygdala Responses

Digging even deeper, in writing this book, I looked at research published by the National Centre for Biotechnology Information (NCBI), part of the U.S. National Library of Medicine (NLM). They had conducted a study of understanding how cognition (perception) is linked to neural function. They studied how the amygdala responds in race-related prejudice.

"There are two [amygdala] one in each hemisphere or side of the brain. This is where emotions are given meaning, remembered, and attached to associations and responses to them (emotional memories)." (Nancy Moyer, 2019)

You may have heard of a fight or flight response, where we make split-second decisions in the heat of a moment. Another term for the fight or flight response is 'An amygdala hijack', which "refers to a personal, emotional response that is immediate, overwhelming, and out of measure with the actual stimulus because it has triggered a much more significant emotional threat. The term was coined by Daniel Goleman in his 1996 book Emotional Intelligence: Why It Can Matter More Than IQ" (NZ, 2020)

Scientists over the last few decades have looked at functional magnetic resonance imaging (fMRI) to study how individuals evaluate, make decisions and respond to race. "It is the amygdala's role in the detection of emotional relevance that inspired the first investigations of its contribution to race processing." (Jennifer T Kubota, 2012)

The Harvard Race Implicit Association Test (IAT) was developed to measure associations between concepts such as good and bad or black and white, etc. The tests, which requires participants to respond very quickly to images, can pick up biases that may not be self-reported or acknowledged. The "magnitude of preference exhibited on the test predicts a host of discriminative behaviors, from nonverbal avoidance to evaluating an individual's work." (Jennifer T Kubota, 2012) A correlation has been identified between implicit responses, such as captured on the IAT and amygdala activity.

Although neural activity to race stimuli can be small, the behavioural responses and their impact can be far-reaching. For instance, "one recent study found that differential brain activity for black and white faces predicts damage awards in hypothetical employment discrimination cases." (Korn H. A., 2012)

The study conducted by the NCBI, did not interpret that amygdala reflects a racial or out-group bias per se, but they argued "that the observed pattern of sensitivity [was] best considered in terms of 'potential threat'. More specifically, [they] argue[d] that negative culturally-learnt associations between black males and potential threat better explain the observed pattern of amygdala activity." (Chekroud, 2014)

So, we can start to see an example of the inequitable way our society operates, and how this dynamic is self-perpetuating, continuing to be driven at implicit, as well as explicit levels. You have a Harvard graduate, calm and articulated man, bird watching in the park, minding his own business. You have a female walking in the park also, who has ingested information which has made her believe she has 'dominant standing' in this world. Their paths crossed, and we saw the loaded interplay which manifested between them.

Again, (as with intergenerational trauma), this element of amygdala responses was a repeated theme which emerged when researching for this book. I, therefore, thought it was important to reference.

Microaggressions

In writing this book and thinking about the fight or flight response, another thing that surfaces, are micro-aggressions. These micro-aggressions are things we often face in the UK. I observe these when looking around at dynamics of how people interact. I observe these when looking at interactions towards myself.

"The American Psychiatric Glossary (eighth edition) defines microaggression as offensive mechanisms or actions by a person that are designed to keep other individuals in an inferior, dependent, or helpless role. This glossary further states that these actions are nonverbal and kinetic and are suited to control space, time, energy, and mobility of an individual (usually non-White or female) while at the same time producing feelings of degradation (APA, 2003). These stunning, automatic acts of disregard stem from unconscious attitudes of racial superiority and may be unintentional (Ridley, 2005). (Bell, 2013)"

To give you a couple of examples of microaggressions. I remember being in a corporate environment within a financial services organisation. I was in the lift, and there happened to be another black male in the lift with me. We were travelling to our respective floors. On the way up the lift stopped, and the lift doors opened, and a white woman was about to step in, bearing in mind we were in a corporate environment, suited and booted. When the lift door opened, the woman visibly recoiled in fear and horror. This was not something she even thought about consciously. This was a response to seeing a black male and a black female in the lift. She obviously felt threatened and fearful.

The woman suddenly seemed to remind herself she was in a 'safe' corporate environment, and she got into the lift. The black man looked at me and rolled his eyes. I shook my head at him. This was a moment between us of shared understanding! We didn't even need any words to articulate what had happened. This was an experience we understood. The woman was projecting her terror and fear onto us, making *us* the problem. It is such a derogatory and insulting way of referring to a person, – to immediately put them into the role of aggressor or attacker. This one experience (of countless) was within a corporate environment! Can you imagine the many day to day interactions? Why should we have to live like this?

Another occasion which comes to mind is one day going to get a pedicure in my local salon. Now I currently live in Brixton. I have lived here for 21 years. We are all familiar with the history of Brixton, the African Caribbean community, the riots in the 1980s and the recent gentrification. Obviously, people have flocked to the area as they like the vibe of the place. However, it seems people want to be in this place, but without the black people in it. I say that because of observing the many microaggressions, which seem to happen in daily experiences.

In the incident which comes to mind, whilst in the nail salon, I was 'relaxing' having a pedicure and at the same time observing the interaction in the store taking place in front of me. There were a group of about 4 or 5 white female customers. They were getting their nails done together, in true girlie bonding fashion. However, there was a black woman in the store. It was clear that this black woman had an established relationship with one of the nail technicians working in the salon. The woman and the nail technician were having a conversation across the room, from their separate places, as is customary at times in nail salons, hairdressers, etc. However, every time the black woman spoke, the group of white females turned as a group to look at her. The looks they were giving were condescending, hostile and questioning. It was almost looking at her as if she were a 'mad' woman. It was immensely powerful, and the energy in the room was palpable. Even I was feeling this implicit energy that they were communicating, that "this woman is a mad woman"!!

Now, as a counsellor, this type of 'listening', is something I have learnt to pay attention to and embrace. It is empathetic attunement, and emotional attunement, using all of your senses to listen and feel? These "nonverbal and kinetic cues" (Bell, 2013), were definitely about controlling the "space, time, energy, and mobility of an individual" (Bell, 2013) (the black woman in the salon). Their actions were certainly successful at "producing feelings of degradation (APA, 2003)" (Bell, 2013) in the salon. This was a horrid display of "disregard" (Bell, 2013). These dynamics of microaggressions, in their different expressions, often happen, across the UK.

Transactional Analysis.

Another theory I thought important to include in this book is transactional analysis.

I think this theory is important to mention as it's a helpful way, when looking at social interactions, to explore our drivers and where our communication is being motivated from. The theory by Eric Berne extends from and has its roots in Freud's psychoanalytical theory, of the unconscious mind.

The theory explores our communications which emanate from our inner relationships between 'Parent', 'Adult' and 'Child' (the three ego states). For example, you may have heard people refer to the voice of the critical inner parent, e.g. 'you're so silly, or why have you done that'?

It can be useful at times for us to take stock and explore the voices of the inner critical parent. These voices never lend support to us. Sometimes if unexplored they can fire away, chastising us in the middle of a presentation, or meeting, or interaction.

These voices are absorbed from authority figures around us when growing. We then take on these messages as a set of thoughts, feelings, attitudes, and behaviours. These messages can play like a tape recorder in the background, and then during that meeting, presentation, or interaction, they start to seek to influence. We can have a side of our parent ego state that is critical, controlling, ordering, fault finding, etc. This would be what is called our '**Controlling** or **Critical Parent.**'

The messages from the parent may not be just critical, fault-finding or controlling, etc. They may in fact, be nurturing messages, and equally included in our set of thoughts, feelings, attitudes and behaviours. This side of our parental ego state might be nurturing, loving and caring and would be seen as our '**Nurturing Parent**.'

Operating out of our parent ego state, whether critical or nurturing, is to put ourselves in a 'parental' position in any interaction.

We also have our adult ego state. The adult ego state operates in the present moment and responds to life around us. This state is involved with rational thinking, questioning, probing, problem-solving, helping, and fact-finding. In this state, we are responsive to life and the world around us and seek to be competent in our reactions.

We then have the child ego state, again with a set of thoughts, feelings, attitudes and behaviours. When we operate out of this state, we access the thoughts and feelings that we felt as a child. As with the parent ego state, we have two streams of the child state. We have the '**Free Child**', where we can be creative, emotional, authentic, playful and expressive. We also have the '**Adapted Child**' ego state, where we can be rebellious, complicit, scared, or dependent.

The ego states within us can be identified on self-reflection, and taking note of where our motivation is coming from can help us to regulate or counter its influence. We all interact at times from different ego states within us. For example:

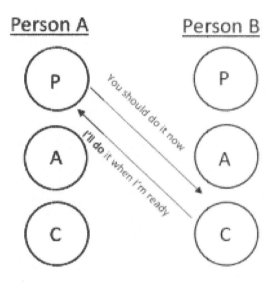

In the above transaction, you have person A operating out of their 'Critical Parent' state, speaking to person B's child state. Person B, then responds out of their rebellious/ 'Adapted Child' state, back to person A's 'Critical Parent state'. This type of interaction would be a parallel transaction. Both people are addressing the ego state from which the other is communicating.

However, there can be what are called crossed transactions, where two people interact towards an ego state the communication has not come from, as per the below.

Person A   ## Person B

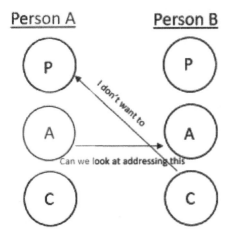

In this example, person A operates out of their adult state to Person B's adult state. However, Person B communicates out of their child state and addresses person A's parent state.

Below is a table of some of the common traits of the different parent, adult and child ego states.

Table 2

Adjectives Strongly Associated with Particular Ego States

Critical Parent	Nurturing Parent	Adult	Free Child	Adapted Child
autocratic	affectionate	alert	adventurous	anxious
bossy	considerate	capable	affectionate	apathetic
demanding	forgiving	clear-thinking	artistic	argumentative
dominant	generous	efficient	energetic	arrogant
fault finding	gentle	fair-minded	enthusiastic	awkward
forceful	helpful	logical	excitable	complaining
intolerant	kind	methodical	humorous	confused
nagging	praising	organized	imaginative	defensive
opinionated	sympathetic	precise	natural	dependent
prejudiced	tolerant	rational	pleasure-seeking	hurried
rigid	understanding	realistic	sexy	inhibited
severe	unselfish	reasonable	spontaneous	moody
stern	warm	unemotional	uninhibited	nervous

(Berne, 1964)

In addition to these three ego states (of parent, adult, child), we have what are called 'Drivers'. Drivers are the ways that we have learnt 'we need to be', when growing up, in order to keep things OK. Some common drivers are:

Be strong, (don't show emotion get on with it);

Be perfect, (make sure things are exactly right);

Please others, (keep others happy at own expense);

Try hard, (never having a feeling of accomplishment, but always trying hard);

Hurry up, (literally do everything fast).

Our drivers then impact on and motivate our interactions. We adopt these drivers when growing up, in response to the adults around us, in order to keep our worlds harmonious.

Now you can imagine the complexities of us operating out of these different states and drivers at different times and its impact on relationships and interactions.

Transactional analysis happens all over the place, in business, in relationships, in interactions. The ideal state would be if we all operated as adult to adult. However, this doesn't always happen. We retreat, and our unconscious ego states get activated in communications. It can be triggering and takes maturity to act at out of an adult state when someone is interacting with you as a critical parent. This would feel undermining, unfair, certainly not about the present time and certainly not a fair response to what you are bringing into the room at that time. I could understand why the child or parent response would be triggered; it would take maturity to stay in the adult state with someone who doesn't want to operate in that way.

You can imagine the different types of interactions that happen across organisations all over the UK when people interact out of these different states.

I had wanted to add this theory to this book, as I think it helps explore unconscious motivations. However, when researching for this book, a theme I had not previously considered began to emerge, and this is the element of the influence of race in transactional analysis. "We cannot understand individuals outside their environment. As Perls (1947/1969) put it, 'There is always an inter-dependency of the organism and its environment' (p. 38)... The problem is, to paraphrase Orwell (1956), that some social factors are more equal than others. Carter (1995), for instance, argues that 'race has been and continues to be the ultimate measure of social inclusion and exclusion ... because it is a visible factor that historically and currently determines the rules and bounds of social and cultural interaction' (p. 3)." (Naughton, 2006)

Research explores how cultural scripting influences the Parent-Adult-Child narratives. Cultural scripting or messages about culture and race can come from family or wider society, e.g. parents, uncles, aunts, grandmothers, teachers, friends, neighbours and media. "In transactional analysis, identity is understood principally in terms of scripting, and cultural identity in terms of cultural scripting. White and White (1975) wrote that 'cultural scripting need not be deliberate or consistent, but merely sufficient to reinforce already habituated patterns established by the family' (p. 171)." (Naughton, 2006)

In their paper on 'Being White' Marie Naughton and Keith Tudor give an insightful example of how cultural scripting may take place in the home, "white cultural scripting fosters a lack of awareness through the messages transmitted to white children in their families of origin, which are also reinforced by the Cultural Parent (Roberts, 1975) in messages such as: 'Least said, soonest mended,' 'We're not responsible ...' (for the slave trade; '2,000 years of patriarchy)', and so on. Through this process of discounting, the white individual is, in effect groomed into a role of bland neutrality and passivity, whereby he or she benefits from his or her privileged place in society yet takes no responsibility for understanding how this status quo has come about. By having little or no conscious awareness of what it means to be white, white people have little or no concept of positive white identity. Thus, white people unconsciously and consciously act out the dynamics and relations of assumed privilege and, at the same time, an incipient guilt and anxiety about white involvement in exploitation and racism." (Naughton, 2006)

Cultural scripting can happen in all families, for example, some of the issues that came up in the focus groups & interviews held for this book, were of families of young black men, trying to build esteem and affirm these young men, and then these men being in a society which counters these messages. Or another theme was conversations families might need to have with their children, to assist them with ways to navigate a society in which there is inequality, similar to conversations African American families might have about how to navigate interactions with the police.

Cultural scripting can also be influenced by societal experiences, such as school, church, books, media, music, where we absorb representations of people being depicted.

Therein internal messages begin to become contaminated and confused, e.g. being given high esteem from family and low esteem from society.

The above is a somewhat overview of the theory, but it gives insight into the different drivers and influences people have when interrelating.

A DIFFICULT PAST

"History is for human self-knowledge....the only clue to what man can do is what man has done. The value of history, then, is that it teaches us what man has done and thus what man is." R. G. Collingwood.

The Triangle of Insight

Is the past something that we celebrate, or is the past something that we forget? Is the past something we are selective about remembering? Or can we learn and grow, from the parts that are not so comfortable to remember?

The past is a hugely important tool for assessing, changing and selecting our choices for the future. In Learning and Development, reviewing past actions, and their outcomes helps us to build on what we feel has been successful, and amend or address any issues that are not taking us towards the desired result.

We can see our dependency on learning from the past, in looking at areas such as medicine, science and scientific research. Even looking just at the subject of applied research, we see the huge benefits gained when we find solutions to problems, which may improve health or develop new technology.

It can be extremely difficult to face the past when events have been traumatic or uncomfortable. However, when our current modus operandi becomes problematic, it can motivate us to seek out better ways of operating.

One of the models we use in psychodynamic counselling, to support clients on their journey of therapeutic healing and change, is called the 'Triangle of Insight'. Using the 'Triangle of Insight', we explore together 'back then', 'out there', and 'in here'.

To take a look 'back then', is to explore the past, and how 'back then' is influencing 'out there', for the client. 'Out there' is the way a client interacts in the world, their choices, influenced by 'back then'.

We include in this exploration also the things taking place 'in here', that is in the therapy room. In this examination, you might find there are patterns of relating learnt 'back then', that are affecting the client's present relationships or perspectives, in their 'out there'. We can examine 'back then' and 'out there' together, with any other issues they might be triggering in the present, ('in here') between therapist and client.

The whole time we are working with the client to address any presenting issues, which may have brought them into the therapy room. As well as exploring their explicit issues, we are also listening out for their implicit voice. What is it that the client is communicating in all they are saying?

Below is a diagram of the 'Triangle of Insight'.

We have explored in the previous chapter, some of the ways we may use to avoid looking at information, which can feel unpleasant to us, or how we unconsciously operate out of implicit knowledge.

Slavery

For the purpose of this book, and examining implicit bias, one of the things I do want to explore, is our difficult shared past, our history of slavery. Whenever this topic is raised, at least before the Black Lives Matter movement, since the killing of George Floyd, this topic is usually avoided, silenced, and muted.

Whenever the painful and impactful history of slavery is mentioned, there is an attempt to distance from and evade the conversation. It is a very difficult past to look at!

However, this past of slavery is so intrinsically and implicitly embedded into the wealth and culture of Britain. I wonder, how do we collectively live with a past that is so uncomfortable to even look at, by its benefactors, and has had such detrimental and far-reaching implications on its recipients. It becomes the collective elephant in the collective room of experience.

We've explored in the previous chapter, how implicit and at times, unpleasant feelings spill out in all sorts of ways such as projection, displacement, etc. I certainly believe this unspoken, unacknowledged, shared past, spills out and influences intercultural interactions in the UK, often.

In researching for this book, I have recently been looking at the work of Professor Catherine Hall. Professor Hall is a British Historian and Academic, whose work is focused on the 18th and 19th centuries. Professor Hall has led the UCL research on 'The Legacies of British Slave Ownership Project.' The project has been a collaborative venture, involving many, including the University of Essex, University of Aberystwyth, University of the West Indies, and several hundred local, regional (economic, cultural and political) and family historians.

In one of her talks on 'The Legacies of British Slave Ownership Project', Professor Hall says: "This is not to do with pointing fingers and saying this person was a nasty slave owner. It's to do with trying to understand the ways we are all implicated in this history, which is a shared history." (Hall, 2013) When referring to the compensation records database @ www.ucl.ac.uk/lbs she says "One of the things that people are discovering, is that all kinds of people who thought they had no connections at all with slave-owning, are discovering that they do have connections, and of course this is a very entangled history between African Caribbean and white British people." (Hall, 2013)

Because this history is so muted, yet the legacy and emblems of it surround us, unacknowledged, it is difficult for us to grasp the extent to which slavery and the history of slavery, influenced culture, country houses, art, financial and commercial institutions, political hierarchy and contemporary thoughts.

Professor Hall says in her talk: "Metropole and colony were inextricably linked, the history of one, inexplicable without the other. The wealth derived from slavery [Eric] Williams demonstrated, was embedded in the social, cultural and political fabric of 18th century Britain. In public schools and Oxbridge colleges, in the town and country houses with their connoisseur's collections amongst the landed, and in the membership of the financial and commercial elite, the older men of the city, the House of Commons and the House of Lords...Williams thesis on the connections between slavery and industrial capitalism has been subjected to decades of critique, but recently the studies of ...Pomeranz, Pat Hudson and others, have reinforced his findings. These arguments have been critical to us, and our findings too, have substantially confirmed while extending his claims." (Hall, 2013)

"Two centuries after the trade was abolished, Britain's economy and cultural heritage remains inextricably tangled with the after-effects of slavery; a tangle which we are only beginning to recognise in full." (Danielle Thom, 2018)

Obviously, we are aware of how awful the practice of slavery was. I recently watched a couple of video tours, of Elmina Castle in Ghana, built by the Portuguese, and Cape Coast Castle in Ghana, built by the British. As we know, the castles became the holding dungeons for captured slaves. Most of the slaves would die from the appalling conditions of being shackled and packed together, with lack of food, lack of light, and at times lack of air, as well of the diseases that ensued from being encased in their own faeces, vomit, urine and menstrual blood. The ones that lived would embark on an ever-decreasing, ever-deteriorating journey on the ships.

The tour guide talked about the arrival of Europeans in Africa, and the strategy to create fractures and wars between tribes. During these inter-tribal wars, people were captured and then sold into slavery. The Europeans then further incentivised these fractions by giving independence to the smaller tribes, who had become part of the larger tribes. The more independent these tribes became, the more they needed weapons to protect themselves. Prisoners of war were then sold on to slavery, to obtain weapons. A self-perpetuating cycle had been implemented. (Paulson, 2018)

In their paper on 'The economic impact of colonialism', Daron Acemoğlu & James Robinson write: "The immense economic inequality we observe in the world today didn't happen overnight, or even in the past century. It is the path-dependent outcome of a multitude of historical processes, one of the most important of which has been European colonialism. Retracing our steps 500 years, or back to the verge of this colonial project, we see little inequality and small differences between poor and rich countries (perhaps a factor of four). Now the differences are a factor of more than 40, if we compare the richest to the poorest countries in the world. What role did colonialism play in this? In our research with Simon Johnson we have shown that colonialism has shaped modern inequality in several fundamental, but heterogeneous, ways." (Daron Acemoğlu, 2017)

Acemoğlu & Robinson talk about how the 'mass colonial project first in the Americas, and then, subsequently, in Asia and Africa' helped to promote institutional and political development and the conditions for the industrial revolution. With conditions in Britain, where parliament and society had "the upper hand" after a struggle with the monarchy, there was "further empowerment of mercantile and industrial groups." (Daron Acemoğlu, 2017) The political institutions and balance of power in Spain were different. In Spain, the monarchy held the power, so political institutions and the economy declined.

In exploring the impact of colonialism on the societies that were colonized, they write "When British colonisers found Latin-American-like circumstances, for example in South Africa, Kenya or Zimbabwe, they were drily capable of, and interested in setting up what we have called 'extractive institutions', based on the control of and the extraction of rents from indigenous peoples. In Acemoglu and Robinson (2012) we argue that extractive institutions, which strip the vast mass of the population of incentives or opportunities, are associated with poverty. It is also not a coincidence that such African societies are today as unequal as Latin American countries." (Daron Acemoğlu, 2017)

There was a report in 2017, based on research and compiled by Global Justice, called 'Honest Accounts 2017: How the world profits from Africa's wealth." The report says "Africa is rich – in potential mineral wealth, skilled workers, booming new businesses and biodiversity. Its people should thrive, its economies prosper. Yet many people living in Africa's 47 countries remain trapped in poverty, while much of the continent's wealth is being extracted by those outside it." (Justice, 2017)

The report then goes on to show how Africa is 'net creditor to the rest of the world.' In 2015 Africa received $161.6 billion in grants, loans and remittances, but credited $203 billion to the rest of the world, "mainly through corporations repatriating profits and by illegally moving money out of the continent, – or by costs imposed by the rest of the world through climate change." (Justice, 2017) This means in 2015, Africa credited the rest of the world $41.3 billion.

So, a self-sustaining system of tribal wars, with the offer of independence, needing weapons to sustain independence and selling prisoners of war, was in operation. We obviously still witness the impact on Africa today, from the extractive institutions model.

The operation of a fractured and divided community was in

place. Slaves were captured and kept in the castles. These people were treated in a barbaric way, and no regard was given for those who would die from the abhorrent treatment, as they were bought cheaply and due to the wars were in constant supply. The journey of the slave got darker as each step progressed. Initially put into dungeons whilst chained together. The majority would die at this stage. Some would in protest go into hunger strike, to die with some dignity. The bodies of those who died were thrown into the sea. Some fought to survive so they could tell their stories. With each dungeon they were moved into, the experience got dimmer.

The female slaves were constantly raped, and females were captured from the age of 13 years old. Women were punished for resisting sexual abuse and made to stand shackled in the sun and rain with no food or water. The governor of the castle would select a woman he wanted to have sex with, and she would be washed publicly by soldiers in the courtyard, to be sent to the governor. When a female got pregnant, she was sent off to have the child. The mixed-raced children were retained and schooled and used as mediators or advocates between the Europeans and Africans.

After leaving the dungeons, the captured people were then packed tightly together onboard a ship. It was not uncommon for someone to wake up chained to someone who had died, or a woman to give birth chained to a dead body.

My father died when I was ten years old. He had a heart attack at home. This was obviously hugely impactful for the family. Our home was full of people who came to mourn when they heard the news. After the funeral, all left, and life went 'back to normal'. As a young child, and in watching the world around me, I felt, 'Oh, we go back to normal now'. However, I hadn't actually dealt with his death, and when I was 18 years old, it came up for me, the pain, the trauma, the hurt. I had to deal with it at 18 years old.

I have lived in my home also for 21 years, a maisonette. In 2019, my neighbour, who had lived downstairs, longer than I, was killed, about 30 mins from home. On hearing the news, I felt traumatised, especially with the thought that I was living on top of all of his belongings. It took me about six months to settle down from the trauma of this news.

I am sure most of us can think of our own relationship to death, or a loved one that has died and the dignity we want to afford them, even in death. Imagine the pain and distress of being chained to a dead person. Imagine the pain of loving and being separated from the people you love, and knowing they are nearby in a dungeon. Imagine knowing your own physical and emotional distress, whilst mourning and wondering about how your loved ones are being treated. Imagine never knowing whether they have died, or the impact of seeing them briefly face to face when you are reunited in a dungeon, before the fate of being put onto a ship.

In the autobiography of Olaudah Equiano, who experienced being a captive slave on a ship, he writes, "The stench of the hold while we were on the coast was so intolerably loathsome, that it was dangerous to remain there for any time, and some of us had been permitted to stay on the deck for fresh air; but now that the whole ship's cargo were confined together, it became absolutely pestilential. The closeness of the place, and the heat of the climate, added to the number in the ship, which was so crowded that each had scarcely room to turn himself, almost suffocated us. This produced copious perspirations, so that the air soon became unfit for respiration, from a variety of loathsome smells, and brought on a sickness among the slaves, of which many died, thus falling victims to the improvident avarice of their purchasers. This wretched situation was again aggravated by the galling of the chains, now become insupportable; and the filth of the necessary tubs, into which the children often fell, and were almost suffocated. The shrieks of the women and the groans of the dying, rendered the whole a scene of horror almost inconceivable..." (Equiano, 1789)

"One day, two of my wearied countrymen who were chained together, preferring death to such a life of misery, somehow made through the nettings and jumped into the sea:... and I believe many more would have done the same if they had not been prevented by the ship's crew, who were instantly alarmed." (Equiano, 1789)

The desperateness of the plight reminds me of the words of Elizabeth Freeman, the first enslaved African American, to win a lawsuit for freedom. "'Any time, any time while I was a slave, if one minute's freedom had been offered to me, and I had been told I must die at the end of that minute, I would have taken it..' Freeman would later say. 'Just to stand one minute on god' airth a free woman–I would.'"(Charles Dickens, 1853)

So, considering the 'Triangle of Insight', we have this shared past, which created an abominable template of human interaction. How has the template of interaction, created back then, influenced the interactions, out there, two centuries later?

In the section, within this chapter, on 'Implicit Motivation', I will talk about the denial and disavowal of this history and explore, the impact of this unconscious information. Also, in the chapter on trauma, I will explore how research shows that this template of interaction became the template for all human relationships, and the ensuing impact of this on us all.

Dehumanisation

Imagine feeling the pain and degradation of the experience of slavery. Imagine being treated as if you were nothing, as if you had no feelings, as if you were non-human.

These people had the most torturous experiences! In amongst the physical and emotional pain and suffering, there was death, groaning, crying, agony, yet they were ignored, they were dehumanised.

"Dehumanisation, so essential to racism, slavery, war and genocide, – is the refusal to recognise the I-amness of other human beings. In other words, empathetic failure characterises not only childhood neglect and abuse, but much other human brutality as well". (Firman F, 1997)

In terms of using the psychodynamic model of the 'Triangle of Insight', I feel this dynamic of seeing a slave, the black person, as less than human, which was so intrinsic to slavery in order to have the disconnection to perform maltreatment, is something we have ingested. This dynamic, coupled with the 'education' around the construction of race, following the abolishment of slavery, plays out implicitly in our society. I will talk more about the introduction of race later in this chapter.

We were all shocked and distressed to see this dynamic of disconnection, from the policeman kneeling on George Floyd's neck, whilst his hands were in his pocket! If we really start to do the uncomfortable work of examining this dynamic, how many slaves could not breathe, in order to support the practice of slavery, which brought huge income into the United Kingdom and influenced our culture. This stuff is really uncomfortable to look at, but do we continue to ignore the dynamics of interaction we have learnt, and have a world where another George Floyd incident could happen? I really hope and pray that the younger generation, the multicultural network of those making a stand and marching for the black lives matter movement, will do a far better job, without the fear of change, which so arrests progress, than we have!

If we continue to look at this uncomfortable dynamic, of the black person dehumanised and the white person in a superior role, how many other black men and women have been shot or killed by the police, both in the US and the UK? How many friends and family members have been left tortured by this, battling against a system that does not see their loved one as important, or worth any justice, – dehumanised?

If we look in the UK, we see this dynamic operating across our organisations, in microaggressions, exclusions, limits on progression, feeling the need to work twice as hard to have the same jobs as white counterparts, often for less remuneration. We also know the disproportionate targeting of black males in stop and search, justified and wrapped up in all sorts of policies.

"Dehumanisation is the process by which conscious and unconscious bias leads people to see a racial minority as less human, – less worthy of respect, dignity, love, peace and protection. Psychology research finds that White police officers and young White students are more likely to see Black children as young as 10 years of age as being less worthy of protection and inviting violence in comparison to White children." (Zevallos, 2015)

I feel the uncomfortable challenge we have landed upon in the UK, is wanting to celebrate the accomplishments of the past, but at the same time wanting to forget or eliminate, how things were accomplished. What happens collectively with all the information we mute?

Through our tangled histories, we have learnt ways of relating, that in wanting to delete the history, have never been addressed. We (black people) are presented as takers from the UK, rather than contributors: through extractive institutions of natural resources in our countries of origin, through sweat and toil of the awful practice of slavery, through the 'apprenticeships' of free labour for seven years after slavery, through contributing to the infrastructure in the UK, whilst facing exclusion and hostility.

Akala writes of the "Great British Contradiction [which] has produced all kinds of conflicting understandings of British history, identity and place in the world, and of who is and is not a citizen or an immigrant." He talks of the "paradox in full effect during what was called 'the Windrush scandal', where the British government deported elderly British citizens 'back' to countries they were not citizens of... those migrants who had really earnt their Britishness by putting up with decades of racism and keeping their heads down, working hard and paying their taxes." He continues to explore the paradox and writes it "was still in full effect here; as Windrush grandparents were being idealised, their grandchildren were being generally portrayed as little more than killers and thieves by the very same organs of the press;" (Akala, 2018)

In using the 'Triangle of Insight', to look back at learnt examples of interaction, we can examine slavery, where we had slave owner and slave. The slave at this time was seen as 'property' and seen as non-human, or dehumanised! Slavery was abolished, and the concept of race was created. With this, Europeans and whites were seen as superior, and blacks and browns were seen as inferior. We then moved to a time of colonialism, where the colonies were seen as possessions or property, and indigenous people were seen as subjugates. We then moved into the time of the British Commonwealth/ Commonwealth in 1917, which was really pulling together the former British territories. The premise of this was that all countries were equal. However, how do you start anew, in forming new ways of interacting ('in here'), between the countries ('out there'), without addressing the shared, powerful history (of 'back then')?

In 1932, the New Commonwealth was founded, of which Winston Churchill became president. "The term New Commonwealth has been used in the UK (especially in the 1960s and 1970s) to refer to recently decolonised countries, predominantly non-white and developing. It was often used in debates about immigration from these countries." (Hennesey, 2004)

Below is a table exploring different events over time and the back then, out there and in here analysis of interactions.

Back Then (The Past)	Out there (Interactions)	In here (Analysis)
Slave Owner/ Slave	Slave seen as property	Slave seen as Non-human
Slavery Abolished	Language of Race Created	Blacks and Brown people seen as inferior
Colonialism	Colonies seen as subjects	Subjects seen as backwards and inferior
Commonwealth	Property	Subjugates
Post War	Subjects invited to UK positioned as unwelcome (immigration)	Subjects invited to UK seen as unwelcome
Current Time	Structural Inequality	George Floyd & many others

In the "'transition from a world of empire to a world of nation-states.' Both the relative freedom from the more extreme forms of segregation, and political repression in the colonies, and the racism that migrants found in the metropole, shaped the development of anticolonial politics. Discrimination in employment, wages, social benefits, and housing was the norm." (MATERA, 2016)

In thinking about this concept, of a learnt mode of interaction which, keeps being reinvented, I think it is interesting to consider the work of the anthropologist Eric E. Wolf and "his discussion of the intersections among colonialism, imperialism, capitalism, slavery, and racism...". Wolf "embedded the slavery driven plantation economy of British North America and the American South firmly within the histories of empire and global capitalism, capturing the central conceptual thrust of the new, widely acclaimed histories of capitalism. Like Edward E. Baptist, he recognized the inbuilt coercive violence of early capitalism when he showed how Africans and Native Americans 'were made to labor in servitude to support a new class of overlords'...and like Sven Beckert and Walter Johnson, he saw a direct link between capitalist expansion, indigenous dispossession, and the rise of imperial states capable of opening markets, enforcing asymmetrical trade relations, and sponsoring webs of exploitation on a global scale." (HAMALAINEN, 2018).

Also, in this context, I find interesting too, the words of Professor Colin Mayer, in a report on the future of the corporation for the British Academy in Nov 2019. "The UK has one of the most extreme forms of capitalism in the world and we urgently need to rethink the role of business in society..." Prof Mayer says that "global crises such as the environment and growing inequality are forcing a reassessment of what business is for." (BBC, 2019)

We have this model of dehumanisation, which has been ingested and become implicit. We have learnt "the affective colonial architecture informing who could feel for whom, in interwar Britain." (MATERA, 2016). People are still being treated as non-human, dehumanized and seen as property to be moved around, when you think of the Windrush scandal and the recent Windrush deportation flight of Jamaicans.

I do not think our responses to this messaging sits at a conscious level, but we internalise this, and it plays out in our society and interactions. For example, I heard you on Good Morning Britain, ask recently, if Madeline McCann were black, would the reaction have been the same? I think we are all aware, whether you want to admit this stuff consciously, or not, that the reaction would not have been the same, if Madeline McCann were black, such is the power of class and race in the UK.

It was quite right that a missing child should, however, be given a great degree of publicity because obviously the family need and want to find their child. Unfortunately, this is not the case for all children! Imagine also the pain if 200 Madelines went missing, and the distress of this on their parents, friends, family and the nation? We were all distressed at the time with seeing pictures of Madeline, and not knowing what had happened to her, having the situation unresolved. When 276 girls, Christian female students, were kidnapped in Chibok in Borno State, the world seemed to look away and continue on with life! The girls were black. What does this communicate about our internal values?

Implicit Motivation

Professor Hall continues in one of her talks: "Anne Laura Stoler has argued, the colonial histories of the European empires, possess unruly qualities. Sometimes they're safely sequestered on the fringes of national histories. Sometimes they erupt into the heartlands, disturbing storeys of unity and progress. Sometimes they are entirely absent, as if empires were simply not there. Not least, she suggests they raise unsettling questions about what it means to know and not know simultaneously. About what is implicit, because it goes without saying, or because it cannot be thought. Or because it can be thought, and is known but cannot be said. Disavowal and distantiation have been crucial mechanisms facilitating avoidance and evasion. To place the slave trade and slavery of the new world, properly back into British history, peopling the silences, speaking what was unspeakable, building on what has already been done and identifying what more there is to do, requires the collective efforts of many. Our work is part of that much bigger collaborative effort towards a new past, one which is both more inclusive and more honest." (Hall, 2013).

We see in the above statement how difficult it is to hold this uncomfortable past consciously. How difficult it can be for any of us to hold uncomfortable information about ourselves, our families, our pasts, unless we have worked through this. The words, "because it can be thought and is known, but cannot be said", illuminates the struggle, of maybe, sometimes, possibly, allowing some knowledge of the unpleasant to be held mentally, but not talked about.

"Disavowal", - so getting into the area of defence mechanisms, such as denial. On the Simply Psychology chart (in chapter 3) we saw that "denial involves blocking external events from awareness. If some situation is just too much to handle, the person just refuses to experience it." There are many other defence mechanisms and ways that we use to avoid facing things that are displeasing. These ways of avoidance sometimes mean projecting our own discomfort onto others.

To give an example of how embedded this stuff is, and how automatically we operate out of it without consideration, I want to look at a recent news story. For me, this shows how deeply entrenched our views are, and how they inform our responses, our feelings, and our choices.

You may remember the story of Corey Lewis, which recently made the headlines in the US. Corey, a black male, runs his own business 'Inspired by Lewis', which is an established youth mentoring program. He regularly takes care of children, as part of his babysitting service, run by his organisation.

One day, Corey was out with two white children, whom he had been sitting for. Whilst out, a white woman saw him, a black male, with two white children and immediately felt suspicious, of why he would be with the children! This woman followed him and challenged him, and in not feeling she had a satisfactory answer, called the police, because he was with the children.

The woman can be heard on the 911 call, reporting to police that she 'had a feeling' something was wrong. This ingested information, she had taken in over a lifetime, which helped her to 'assess' this situation, was so informative, it instinctively caused her to have 'a feeling' that something was wrong!

This shows the depth of this implicit conditioning and its motivation on actions. The woman's emotions and mind were responding to the external stimuli of seeing a black man with two white children. I am sure we can agree there were all sorts of suppositions and assumptions taking place in the woman's response.

I mentioned earlier about the impact of negative culturally-learnt associations, between black males and potential threat, on amygdala activity (Chekroud, 2014). In seeing a black male with two white children, this woman sees a perceived threat. Her emotions are responding, informing her 'I have a feeling'. How learnt and loaded is this response, all to a man running his established business.

I mentioned in the opening of this book, how I had one day shared with my peers my experiences around racism, at the beginning of counselling training. It was the time we had an amazing connection as a group, which some called 'magical', some called 'spiritual'. I was the only black peer at the time.

On the course, at the start of each lesson, we would have a 'check-in' where each person talks about how they are feeling, and what might be taking place for them either personally or in relation to the training. Because of my connection with this group and because of the way I was feeling, I had decided I was going to share with them the way I was feeling about racism, and living in the UK. I was at a point where I was feeling particularly fed up, stressed and upset. I was upset with all the interactions I observed towards myself and towards other BAME people, I was upset with the experience. I was finding it weary, draining, grating, and arduous.

It's interesting, because these experiences, this knowledge of shared understanding around issues of race and the way you are treated, is understood by other BAME people. For example, at the weekend, during a family conversation about race, due to seeing images about the Black Lives Matter movement on TV, we had a conversation about experiences in the UK. My niece talked of going shopping to Bluewater with her white friend and white friends mother and (when walking with her white friend's mother) seeing lots of people staring at her, as if to say, why are you with her?

My brother-in-law shared his experiences of the sauna in the gym, and how when he enters; the white men leave soon after. Or if he's in the sauna, they open the door and say, 'it's hot in here mate' and then close the door without entering. He concluded; he gets to have saunas by himself.

Do these experiences around race mean you cannot have a good life, good days or diverse friends, not at all, but in the midst of it all, remains this poison, which is so draining! For me it is normative, and something you manage and can articulate with other BAME people (although with the construction of race there are varying degrees in the way we are regarded and treated). However, in doing interviews and focus groups for this book, when considering how implicit bias manifests in our systems, it was educational for me. I spoke to a couple of professionals, who were not born in the UK, they were in fact born in Africa. They educated me that they never had issues around race, or self-esteem. They did not know they were 'black' until they came to this country/ the US. It was there they were educated about 'who they were' in the eyes of the majority. It was there they started to face battles around progression, self-esteem, etc. This is a theme I am starting to hear, that BAME people abroad do not go through the crushing struggles around identity and suppression, that we face in the UK/ US.

So, on this particular day, I was already feeling really upset and unhappy. I was also tired as I had left the 'friendliness of working in the city as a black woman', (I am being sarcastic here), and done a 2-hour commute across London to my course. When I arrived at the centre, I walked into the room where the course was usually held and it was empty, apart from a woman on a ladder, sticking a banner onto the wall with blue tac. This woman was white, and I think it is important to mention her colour for this story.

Now, as I say this was at the start of my training. My course has helped me to shift in the way I process issues of racial oppression, although obviously, it is still upsetting. Possibly if this were a great day, I could have bounded across the city, feeling amazing. However, such is the draining experience of living with systemic racism at times, on top of all the other life issues we all have, it is impacting.

The room was empty, and I was thinking, where are my coursemates? I then asked the woman – "is the counselling course not taking place in here today?". The woman gave me a very condescending look and said (very abruptly) "Sorry?". In noting her look, noting the way I had been feeling, and noting she was responding in a very unfriendly tone, I said "it's OK", and decided I would go and look for my class in the centre.

However, the woman then proceeded to ask me "who are you"? In fact, I would say her entire condescending look communicated that question to me, "who are you, and what are YOU doing here"? I then said to her, "you don't need to know who I am." Now, this interaction between us, admittedly was not the friendliest of communications. I could have simply told her who I was and diffused the situation. However, at the time, in already feeling very upset around issues of race and racism, and in observing the woman and her facial expressions and tone, I picked up that this woman was seeing me as an 'intruder' in the centre. I sensed that this woman was feeling fear, and the normal response would have been to pacify her fears and show that I am harmless. However, in my upset, at the time I felt, you know what, I am not going to pacify your fear! In fact, I am going to leave you with your fear, for you to process this.

It seemed this woman did not trust that I had a legitimate reason for being there, and she wanted clarity around this. In reflecting back, it was not unreasonable for someone to ask another person who they are, if entering an organization. However, this 'who are you' was so loaded with suspicion. It did not feel like 'can I just clarify your details and then I can show you to where you should be', it felt like 'what are you doing here'. As they say, it is not what you say, but the way that you say it.

I then left the room, and the woman got off the ladder and began following me through the centre to ascertain who I was. I then bumped into my peers; they could see me looking frazzled with a woman who was now very angry following me. I stopped and asked them where the course was today. The woman went over to one of my white peers, whom she had never met, and then began complaining about me, as if my peer was the tutor. There was immediately a relationship of regard and trust with my white peer, but suspicion and mistrust with me. Both my peer and I had paid the same tuition fee to study the same course. As my white peer later said, the woman 'was making all sorts of incorrect assumptions, seeing me as the tutor'.

As I say, now after the training, and on reflection, I could have responded differently at the time, and diffused the situation. However, how many times can you carry and manage another person's projections and judgement towards you? Projections and judgements which are so demeaning. Even when you are calm and complicit, situations still have unfavourable outcomes.

I go back to the Corey babysitter situation, and the instinctive response of the woman who had 'a feeling'. Imagine these automatic, embedded responses and 'feelings' when making decisions about job applicants, sometimes with 'foreign' sounding names'. Imagine the 'feelings' that are triggered, feeling something is not right, the amygdala responses, that trigger actions, all from the information we have been conditioned into believing. Imagine the assumptions people make on a one on one basis, leading to the doors that are either opened, or the doors that are closed to a person.

As I talked about in the previous chapters, no human wants to run towards pain; we naturally want to run away from discomfort. It is hugely challenging to face difficult or unpleasant areas of ourselves. Usually, we need an impetus to force us to do so.

I talked previously about facing an MS scare, and when things reached this level, making some extremely uncomfortable decisions to minimize stress in my life. Similar to the tough counselling journey, I have to say the benefits of processing through that change, far outweighs the losses and consequences. The feeling of peace and a clear conscience far outweighs any stress.

I am sure many of us can think of a romantic relationship in our past, that did not work out. Sometimes, the issues, that may have caused the ending, were right there from the beginning. We see things, but we allow ourselves not to notice. We overlook or make excuses for events. It's when we get to a place to 'allow' ourselves to see, when we are 'ready' to see, that we begin to allow ourselves to accept the things we previously could not. At this stage, we can reel off a list of issues that were there right from the very beginning. At this stage, we can agree with the observations of family, friends, and others. We can allow ourselves to see.

There can be so much going on in our lives, that we are aware of, but do not allow ourselves to acknowledge. As a counsellor, I know how effective making connections with the past are for moving forward with the future. The power of the unacknowledged literally influences the present, but unaddressed.

The 'Hierarchy' Of Race

As I alluded to in chapter 2, Information Download, race is a social construct. There is much research that shows this. If you take a moment to think, it's incredible how divisive it is for all of us, to have a hierarchy based on race. It is quite unbelievable that we operate in this way.

To have a hierarchy of race, pits us against each other, considering in reality that we are all equal. It causes the people at the top of the hierarchy to feel a sense of superiority, entitlement and a sense that those 'lower down the chain' are inferior, or possibly a sense of being altruistic, for supporting those 'lower down the chain'. For those in the middle, they may sometimes feel, they are not as bad as those 'lower down the chain', and a sense of regard or aspiration for those 'higher up the chain'. They have historically, been used by those at the top of the chain, as mediators, to reach those at the bottom. We see this with the mixed children born into slavery and will see later in this section, how Indians were used as intermediaries for Africans after the abolishment of slavery. For those at the bottom of the chain, there is the ever-internal battle of instilling internal self-esteem, whilst constantly fighting against those in the middle and higher end of the chain, treating them with lack of regard.

All the time, this hierarchy creates disharmony and conflict.

At times I think, imagine if Aliens were watching us from another planet, watching us live in a beautiful world yet warring against each other and causing such harm to the environment. We have the opportunity of life on this planet, yet instead of working together for the benefit of the planet and all, we live selfishly.

When astronauts view the earth from space, they have an experience called 'the overview effect', where they feel a state of "'inexplicable euphoria', a 'cosmic connection...' On March 6th, 1969, Rusty Schweikart experienced a feeling that the whole universe was profoundly connected... Two years later, Apollo 14 astronaut, Edgar Mitchell (joint record holder with Alan Shepard for longest ever Moon walk of 9 hours and 17 minutes) reported experiencing an 'Overview Effect'. He described the sensation gave him a profound sense of connectedness, with a feeling of bliss and timelessness. He was overwhelmed by the experience. He became profoundly aware that each and every atom in the Universe was connected in some way, and on seeing Earth from space he had an understanding that all the humans, animals and systems were a part of the same thing, a synergistic whole. It was an *interconnected euphoria*. Schweikart and Mitchell's experiences are not isolated anomalies, many other astronauts since the 1970's have reported this Overview Effect." (Today, 2008)

In one of her talks on 'The Legacies of British Slave Owner-ship Project', Professor Hall talks about the Kingsley brothers. Charles Kingsley was a writer, intellectual, historian, Clergy-man, novelist, socialist reformer and member of the Victorian intellectual elite. She also talks about his brother Henry Kings-ley, the novelist.

Professor Hall talks of the huge settler explosion that was tak-ing place in the 1830s, where white West Indian families saw the West Indies would no longer be profitable and began mov-ing to Canada, Australia, New Zealand and the Cape.

The talk tells of how these influential brothers, would write about their experiences overseas and how these representa-tions of the countries, their voyages, their descriptions of em-pire and indigenous people were 'percolated' through these brothers writing.

The descriptions of Henry Kingsley's representation of the Abo-riginal people in Australia were ugly, in his writing "They're savage, they're barbaric, they're hopeless, they're ugly." This is against the comparison of "the beautiful blond white set-tlers." (Hall, 2013)

After the emancipation of slavery, the problem faced was who the labour force would be, as it was now difficult to use the Afri-cans. The answer was seen as bringing large numbers of "Indian indentured labourers" into Trinidad and Guyana. (Hall, 2013) This is why the population in both places are half and half of Af-ricans and South Asians.

So, in trying to think through the 'hope' for the future of Guy-ana and Trinidad, Charles Kingsley argues that "'the real hope for this country is more white migrants. What we need is more people like those men who settled in the past.' Kingsley was thinking of men like him, 'men who would do the hard work, and discipline their neighbour and organize themselves.' He says that they could be 'little centres of civilization, for the rest of the society.'" (Hall, 2013)

So in establishing a "'hierarchy of how people might function in this society', the next layer down from the white leaders, would be the 'Indians', the 'Coolies' as everyone called them, because 'Coolies' he thought 'were much more industrious and docile than Africans. They came from a society which had been civilized. It was stagnant…its civilization was long, long ago, but they could be rescued. It was true they had terrible superstitions and ridiculous religious beliefs, but…there was more hope of rescuing them.'" (Hall, 2013)

At the bottom of this hierarchy, were placed black people, which the "'Coolies would educate…and bring them slowly, slowly, slowly into civilization.'" (Hall, 2013)

Kingsley's final book At Last tells "the story of the hierarchy of races, with whites as the civilizing agents, Coolies as the next layer down, and Africans as the ones who might, might, might eventually enter civilized society fully…These are the stories which the Kingsley Brothers are telling, not just the British public, but a global public. These books sell large numbers in Australia, in United States and so on. These are the ways in which slave owning families are passing on stories about what race means. These are the reconfigurations of racial thought, which are going on in the period after emancipation and which demonstrate to us how nothing ended with abolition. Something else happened, but the something else left huge legacies of inequality which we are still living with today and we still need to address." (Hall, 2013)

So if we are to start tapping into dynamics of regard and disregard, into value and lack of value, into attitudes around race, which is a social construct, then it's good to explore our early messages around race, and where these came from.

We see these prominent and influential British men travelling the world, and 'educating' the UK, the United States and Australia about the places they had been to and the indigenous people that lived in these places. From their education, we learn that white people are superior, Asians are the next level down, and black people are at the bottom.

What has happened with all of the information the UK, the US, and Australia has embedded around race? Have these hierarchies and views suddenly diminished, or have they become 2nd nature? I would argue that they very much still exist and are present, including in systemic structure and press reporting. This creates an ever-self-perpetuating cycle of feeding these inequalities and untruths. This hierarchy is very much evident in daily interactions and in our institutions.

I am sure we can all relate to things becoming 2nd nature when we think of something such as learning to drive a manual car. I remember my first couple of driving lessons, learning about the brake first (which the instructor also had control of), then the gear stick, the clutch, the steering wheel, the hand brake, the mirrors. My instructor broke it all down for me, how everything worked. I remember in my first lesson, driving the car. I was driving, but to be honest, I didn't have a clue about how it was all happening. I hadn't yet embedded it into my mind.

I remember going home and going through all the steps, one by one in sequence, cover the clutch and brake, then get the biting point with the accelerator, take the hand brake off, push down on the accelerator and lift up on the clutch, as well as the signalling, mirror and manoeuvring. I'm sure we have all been through this process but learnt in our unique ways. However, how many of us experienced drivers even think about the biting point, or the accelerator, or any of the things we may have struggled with initially when learning to drive? Driving is now so embedded; we are so comfortable, we can have conversations, listen to the radio, use the sat nav, all whilst driving. It is now second nature, as most learning becomes with practice.

In looking at the vast amount of research there is on the construction of race, I came across an interesting paper by the Anthropologist Professor Audrey Smedley, Published in the American Anthropologist. In her paper, she says "Race as a mechanism of social stratification and as a form of human identity is a recent concept in human history. Historical records show that neither the idea nor ideologies associated with race existed before the seventeenth century." (SMEDLEY, 1999)

Professor Smedley goes on to write "When 'race' appeared in human history, it brought about a subtle but powerful transformation, in the world's perceptions of human differences. It imposed social meanings on physical variations among human groups, that served as the basis for the structuring of the total society." She talks about the 18th century during which time, "the English began to have wider experiences with varied populations and gradually developed attitudes and beliefs that had not appeared before in Western history, and which reflected a new kind of understanding and interpretation of human differences. Understanding the foundations of race ideology is critical to our analysis." (SMEDLEY, 1999)

Professor Smedley continues to write, that "for the English settlers, 'savagery' was an image about human differences that became deeply embedded in English life and thought, and provided a foil against which they constructed their own identity as 'civilized' Englishmen. They brought this image of what savagery was all about with them to the New World, where it was soon imposed on the native populations...Savagery carried with it an enormous burden of negative and stereotypic characteristics, grotesquely counterposed against the vision that the English had of themselves as a civilized people. *Every new experience...widened the differences and denigrated all other peoples who were not part of the civilized world.*" (SMEDLEY, 1999)

In referencing some of the more recent associations in History to these created stereotypical characteristics, Winston Churchill, national icon ingested some of these descriptions of 'the other' in that he "did not really think that black people were as capable or as efficient as white people". (Toye, 2011) And he "accepted contemporary ideas of Anglo-Saxon superiority 'unquestioningly'". (Toye, 2011)

"The problems that this has entailed, especially for the low-status 'races', have been enormous, immensely complex, and almost intractable. Constant and unrelenting portrayals of their inferiority conditioned them to a self-imagery of being culturally backward, primitive, intellectually stunted, prone to violence, morally corrupt, undeserving of the benefits of civilization, insensitive to the finer arts, and (in the case of Africans) aesthetically ugly and animal-like." (SMEDLEY, 1999)

However, we have been left with the embedment of this social construct and the hierarchy of race, which implicitly authorizes day to day interactions, economic power, and opportunities.

In thinking about some of the practical ways this has played out in the UK over the last 50 or so years, I remember stories my 95-year-old uncle has shared with me. For most of his life, he has been the most generous and loving man whenever I have interacted with him. For the larger part of his life, he has been an active and agile man. In his 70s he was still getting up on his roof to do repairs, as he has told us. During his late 80s / early 90s he lived independently, still cooking and cleaning, as most of his generation, his wife, including his Dr had already passed. Even in his 90s, he is still able to remember everyone's names, and their information.

On one occasion, during a visit to see him with my sister, nieces, and cousins' children, - he opened up about his experiences when he came to this country. He talked about the hostility. The fact that the National Front would post papers on fire through your letterbox, and they would chase you. He spoke about how hostile the environment was. At the time he spoke to his local mayor/ MP, who was unsupportive and basically told him to put up with it. He determined he would not!

As we know many of our parents ('Afro-Caribbean'), who arrived in this country, who were invited to this country as they were needed to support the infrastructure and economy after the 2nd world war, were greeted in a very hostile way. Many of them had established qualifications and careers, which were 'not recognised' in this country. They either had to retrain, to do something else, or take a menial, unqualified role! Not that their abilities were any different to the British, but though invited, they encountered barriers.

In the hostility, thankfully at the time, there was a community spirit of sticking together. Many of them lived together and saved to buy their own homes. They devised the 'pardoner' system, where a group of people would join together and each person saving, would contribute a designated amount of money each month, which was collected by the organiser of the 'pardoner'. Each member of the group would receive funds collected at the rota'd time. This would be rotated across the group.

They found ingenious ways of saving, innovative ways of purchasing homes, ingenious and supportive communities. They had to find creative systems of survival in a country where often they were not included or supported.

Since that time, there have been huge strides made to eradicate people posting such overt signs in windows as no dogs, no blacks, no Irish. Many rights were fought for and introduced, including positive discrimination which allowed for some inclusion. At times there seems to be the rhetoric that if you do make it and are successful, then you have only reached that position due to an equal opportunities' quota, and not your capability. Whilst we are talented, if there isn't positive discrimination, we will remain forever excluded.

I note that for a long time, after the boom of the 80s and 90s, BAME people were just not on British TV. It's as if we did not exist, including in the COVID-19 reporting of NHS staff, which generally showed all-white staff. If ever there was a deception, to me, this was it. I live in London, and I cannot recall a time where I have ever entered a hospital and seen only white staff. Yet during this time, the 'heroes' were all white. There was a report that showed 'heroes' during the pandemic, including a bin man, a bus driver, and staff from the NHS. Again, not one single one of these represented were BAME.

However, if we take the template embedded in literature in the UK, the America's and Australia, of the hierarchy of the civilising white people, the 'docile' coolies in the middle and Africans at the bottom, "who might, just might be civilised" (Hall, 2013), it fits well with the representation of white hero's during the COVID-19 pandemic, and elimination of any BAME contribution.

The times we were represented, were when we were presented as people who were four times more likely to die from COVID-19, than white people. Inequality and the way we are systemically treated, was not initially mentioned in this reporting. In fact "third-party submissions, which reportedly highlighted structural racism and social inequality, were left out of the government-commissioned report" (Guardian, 2020). To me, it's akin to saying cakes are four times more likely to burn, than bread. But omitting the fact the baker is leaving cakes in the oven for an hour longer than they should be.

I wonder, if there is a physiological reason why we are four times more likely to die from COVID-19, why we are not dying in mass from COVID-19 in the Caribbean and Africa? I would say the statistics need to factor in the relationship of the UK with BAME people, and the systemic inequalities that exist.

We have heavily invested into the UK. Not only have we heavily invested, but we also were not welcomed and to many extents it seems still are not, with the resurfacing of the immigration debate, the sending home of the Windrush people, many of whom had invested in the communities in Britain, and cut ties with their homeland. Many of whom came to the UK as children to build the communities and then were returned to places they had no links with, given no regard and sent 'home'.

In having to endure systemic inequalities, there are the psychological and health impacts, which I will expand more on in the chapter on 'Trauma'. I will also explore more of what research says about the disparities which influence health outcomes, in the chapter on COVID-19.

Filtered History & the Complexities that Brings

So, we had the horrific killing of George Floyd, which the world witnessed. People were so impacted by his killing, that in the middle of a pandemic, a global movement was set in motion, where people were protesting, standing against what they had witnessed. It was quite moving to see images of thousands of multicultural people, kneeling in solidarity outside St. Georges Hall in Liverpool, to symbolize how strongly they felt. They were prepared to go through the discomfort, of kneeling on hard pavements or surfaces, resisting the urge to shift into a more comfortable position.

We also saw Nancy Pelosi kneeling, to the point where she was then struggling to stand up afterwards. All over the world people were demonstrating, how powerfully they were impacted by seeing a policeman kneeling on another man's neck, for 8 mins and 46 seconds, in such a detached way his hands were in his pocket. Obviously, choosing to kneel on a pavement, comes in no way near the agony and distress George Floyd must have felt. Kneeling was a symbolic gesture of protest.

We were in the middle of a pandemic. In the UK, we were still under a 'lockdown'. However, people were so moved, they came out, they took risks of standing in crowds, to show they were against what they had seen.

Suddenly, in the UK, during the Black Lives Matter protests, we began to see statues being toppled, removed, and thrown into the river. Suddenly the debate began to shift from George Floyd to a focus on statues.

We saw the statue of Edward Colston thrown into the river. We saw the statue of Winston Churchill defaced. We saw policeman surrounding and protecting the statue of Churchill. We heard debates on TV of 'what is next', 'where does this end'? We saw posts on social media saying, 'leave our statues alone', 'they are our statues', 'our history', 'if you don't like it then leave'.

We started to be educated about the statues. We then saw a group of white male's march into London to protect the statues. We saw the iconic picture emerge of Patrick Hutchinson, a black man, carrying an injured white protestor, who had gone to defend the statues, which went viral. We then saw a picture emerge of a man who had gone to 'protect the statues', urinating on the statue of PC Keith Palmer. This then caused huge national outrage, around the lack of respect and honour for PC Keith Palmer. The man, Andrew Banks, was later arrested and charged. He attended to protect the statues but admitted he didn't know which ones. "He did not know which ones!" (Independent, 2020)

Suddenly, the debate shifted from the upset of a man's life being snuffed out, in public daylight, and the pain of seeing a policeman have no regard for a black man's life, to focusing the attention on statues. Suddenly, in the debate, all our awareness is turned to these figures, that are dotted and erected all over the UK. These symbols of history that are all around us, which we walk past daily, yet remain oblivious of. Suddenly these symbols are in the forefront.

I wonder, was it really about the symbols, or was it our respective relationship to these symbols and what they represented, that fueled the debate? Suddenly we were all starting to see, the symbols erected around us all, that we had not been aware of.

We have a History that has been edited and presented with narratives, but our connections and emotions to the 'known' history remain. There are huge complexities in collectively facing the truth and reality of our shared history.

On the one hand, you have the trauma which has happened as part of slavery. Trauma does not just stay with one generation, it evolves into intergenerational trauma, and there is also evidence to show that the past creates epidemiological changes, which impacts the present, – as per the work of Professor Kimberley Theidon (Medical anthropologist). There are therefore entire generations, living with the impact of the colonial and slavery past of Britain.

We also have the historical hierarchy of race, which is unspoken, but we see very much evident in the demographics of institutions in the UK today. How many organizational charts map the hierarchy of race?

There are also huge financial disparities, where BAME people are generally excluded from wealth - see Durable Inequality Theory by Charles Tilly, in the chapter on how this manifests in our systems, and also the extractive institution's models, which operate in countries of which BAME people may have historical connections.

On the other hand, also due to the *actual* history coupled with the *narratives* of history told, you have the contrast of institutional access to resources generally given to white people, because of structural inequalities (see Durable Inequality Theory again by Charles Tilly), also the compensation from slavery paid to many, including annuities, and property.

This is not about apportioning blame at all and is certainly not about overlooking the many personal hurdles that we all face, regardless of race! Because you are white does not mean that you have had a struggle-free life, or because you are black had an awful life, far from it, and is not the purpose of this book. What I am trying to do in this book is understand and map the macro picture, that creates a culture where there can be such an event as George Floyd, and the other countless men and women that have been killed by police before him, as well as identifying additional processes, that support structural inequalities.

"Racial group membership is consistently traced to inequitable outcomes on every indicator of quality of life, and these outcomes are well documented and predictable (Hughes & Thomas, 1998; Williams, 1999). Limiting our analysis to the *micro* or individual level prevents a macro or big picture understanding. At the micro level ('I didn't own slaves'), we cannot assess and address the macro dimensions of society that help hold racism in place, such as practices, policies, norms, rules, laws, traditions and regulations" (Robin DiAngelo & Ozlem Sensoy, 2017)

Also, on the other hand, in addition to the above, you have the 'known' history, coupled with the deeply embedded love for the country, the UK. This country that has built a huge empire. There is pride in the empire, that goes so deeply to the core, to the very heart. There is the impact of generations of pride being embedded and ingested, influencing the family line and perspectives. It is a deep pride, the British lion's roar, that is so intrinsic in people.

I remember one day going to watch the American theatre show Hamilton, in London at the Victoria Theatre. There was such a hype about the show, the tickets were really hard to obtain, and we were told to arrive early. As advised, on arrival, the queue was sprawling around the theatre.

Even though the show was about Hamilton, and his impact as one of the founding fathers of the US, the character King George III featured in a supporting role in the play. However, this was being viewed in London, and every-time 'King George III' would appear on stage, the audience erupted in applauds. By the end of the show, the audience were erupting in a roar, at 'King George III', every time he appeared. This was not just about regular applauds, but it seemed more about pride, history, identification, belonging, tribalism, etc.

The national pride was captured also in the film The Darkest hour. At the end of the film, where Churchill makes his infamous, stirring, galvanizing speech, 'we will fight them on the beaches, we will fight them on the streets', the moment is captured by an enormous roar, the roar of pride, territory, nationalism, honour and determination to fight for Britain.

In even beginning, to look collectively at the past, we have an array of elements in the mix, such as: trauma, pride, pain, torture, anguish, ease, fear, hostility, anger, allegiance, to name a few. How do we collectively, face beginning to look differently at our history? The past that has always been around us, shown through these symbols, which we have been unaware of. The past, hanging just out of sight of consciousness. The past, that has so shaped the present, whether that be in wealth, prosperity, open doors, trauma, pain and struggle. There are complexities in beginning to look at a past that has been edited.

"The Slavery business had huge tentacles in British society. It's not just the plantation owners, (the absentees as they were called who lived here, and were living off the fruits of that business), it's also the people involved with navy, shipbuilding, sugar refining, metal manufacturer, toy manufacture, textiles, finance capital. We can trace all the ways in which the slavery business, the tentacles of it went deep into British society...So not a superficial matter at all, employing (as the slave owners wanted everyone to know) hundreds of thousands of people in different ways" (Hall, 2013)?

The slave owners were "rarely remembered, once the heyday was over,...the slave owners abandoned [their] identity and re-created themselves, as simply metropolitan men....unsullied by connections with slavery" (Hall, 2013)

So, we have this huge past that has shaped the finance, culture, and infrastructure of the UK. Yet, the way in which our finance, culture and infrastructure was influenced has been forgotten. The past of slavery that was so instrumental to the operation and income of Britain has been wiped out. As Professor Hall says, the identities abandoned and recreated. Instead, we live with a distorted version of history.

We remember Britain as being instrumental in the abolishment of slavery, but we do not talk about the compensation of slave owners, which was a negotiated part of the act of abolishment. We do not focus on the huge payout afforded to slave owners, paid by the British taxpayers, the debt of which was only fully paid in 2015. Many of us are aware of the tweet by HM treasury in 2018, which said "Here's today's surprising #FridayFact. Millions of you helped end the slave trade through your taxes", which was swiftly deleted.

However, such is the promoted and embedded view of Britain's relationship to slavery, that we are seen as having an altruistic involvement, rather than the contrasting reality. Instead of an honest truth, we are educated with narratives, which mirror the hierarchy of race, the stories told of 'heroes' at the top of the pyramid and villains at the bottom.

Also, with the romantic view of empire, it eliminates the brutality that accompanied conquest, and the stories we are never told. I was educated recently about Sir Evelyn Baring, recipient of the Order of St Michael and St George, the highest award given to British officials who work abroad. Sir Evelyn Baring was the great grandfather of Mary Wakefield, wife of Dominic Cummings. "Sir Evelyn Baring was Governor of Kenya when Kenya was a colonial possession of the United Kingdoms, and while he was there in the 1950s, he instituted a system of concentration camps, which even his own attorney general, compared to those run by the Nazi's. He drove into these concentration camps...almost the entire population of the Kikuyu people, then numbering over a million people. Huge numbers died, some of them of starvation and disease, many beaten to death, burnt to death, tortured to death...Before Britain left Kenya, there was an order sent down...to conduct what they called a thorough purge of the archives." (News, 2020)

Rather than being shown the reality of Africa, financing the world through the extractive institutions model, we are shown images of poor African's, poverty, a broken infrastructure, and the world giving aid to Africa, whether that be through charitable causes or BBC's children in need. Research by the GIGA Research Programme (German Institute of Global and Area Studies) states "Even beyond the aftermath of (neo) colonialism, and notwithstanding continuing deficits in good government in many African countries, the EU bears responsibility for the fragile state of many African economies. The self-interested trade policies of the EU and other world powers contribute to poverty and unsatisfactory development in SSA [Sub-Saharan Africa]. This threatens to perpetuate asymmetrical power relations in the new Economic Partnership Agreements (EPAs), to the detriment of regional integration and pro-poor growth." (Kohnert, 2008)

The research does go on to state however, that "mounting competition between China and other global players for Africa's resources is resulting in windfall profits for Africa. The latter is leading to a revival of seesaw politics, already known from the times of the Cold War, on the part of African states. This could be profitable for Africa's power elite, but not necessarily for Africa's poor." (Kohnert, 2008)

So implicit and embedded is this view of poor Africa & African's, in the psyche, it seems to keep people elevated above their own situations, so if they wish to feel better about their circumstances, they can think – "it's not as bad as a starving person in Africa". Or if a person wishes to hurt a black person in an argument, they retreat to the words of "go back to Africa".

I can recall occasions where Africa has come up in conversations as the worst-case scenario, the setting a person would not like to be in, a scenario which they can use as an apparent "weapon" to throw perspective on an argument. For example, I recall being, not so long ago with a long-term friend of mine, who also happens to be black. I was in her home, with her now ex-husband, who happened to be white, as I had gone to visit them for the day. At one point, we got into a robust discussion between us, and we were each sharing our perspectives on the issue. I hadn't realised her husband was becoming a little irate. He then stood up and said, "oh well, there are people starving in Africa", as an attempt to make his final point on the argument, and left the room.

I remember being flabbergasted and thinking, what on earth, has Africa, got to do with our conversation? It was not even related to what we were talking about. To me it felt like, I disagree with what you are saying, I am uncomfortable with our conversation and I do not feel I am coming out ahead, so in my frustration, I will use my hidden tool of Africa, to 'put you in your place'! I can assure you, this is not the only time this dynamic has been used.

To me, it reminds me of the dynamic in close relationships, where a person knows where the weak spots are, and how to hurt the other person. However, I feel in these scenarios, what is happening is that people are using learnt narratives about race, which become implicit, whether they wish to admit it or not. When the pressure is on, when the heat is on, these 'insults' come out, as an attempt to hurt a person, as a learnt weapon, such is the implicit information that we have learnt.

We have a history, which is framed on celebrating British heroism, and this is the lens through which things are often positioned. Where history might show Britain in a bad light, it is muted and erased. A recent example of this, to me is the COVID-19 death toll reporting. When our death tolls were behind Italy and Spain, we were continually comparing, mapping our progression, the government referring to us as 'exemplars'. However, when our death rate started to overtake Italy and Spain, we were told, not to compare. Suddenly the daily death reporting was taken away from the focus on the news agenda.

We have a history where BAME inventors and heroes are erased, muted and forgotten. We have a narrative instead of BAME citizens as villains, terrorists, committing knife crime, criminals, etc. Our contributions are erased.

The race of a white person is not mentioned in news reporting; it is seen as the norm, normalized. The race or religion of a BAME person is mentioned in relation to news when the story is negative, which I will cover more in 'The Press, The Messages continue'. This dynamic seems in keeping with the embedded differences created with the social construct of race and the "negative and stereotypic" (SMEDLEY, 1999) traits assigned to 'the other'.

As Dr Francis E. Kendall writes, "For those of us who are white, one of our privileges is that we see ourselves as individuals, 'just people', part of the human race. Most of us are clear, however, that people whose skin is not white are members of a race". (Kendall, 2002)

"Throughout human history there have been numerous examples of the ways in which 'the other' has been projected out and demonized. Indeed, the history of madness-and sanity-is the history of the projection of people's fear and society's exclusion of the unknown...The dominant norm is not so studied;

it is assumed. In this sense it is not surprising that the personal meaning and significance of 'race' has not been applied to white people: 'Those in the dominant group have little awareness of their position as being white, or able-bodied, or heterosexual, etc. 'Norm' therefore, somehow, remains unquestionable, not worthy of exploration, indeed out of awareness' (Lago & Smith, 2003, p. 7)." (Naughton, 2006)

Unfortunately, as BAME people, we don't get the privilege of being seen as individuals, – we are usually grouped together. Akala, in an interview with James O'Brien, touched on the subject of 'collective blame', (which I feel is something that is projected onto us (as part of a collective defence mechanism, that comes with evading the entirety of history)). He talks about the "lunacy of ethnically targeted stop and search which...doesn't help solve the problem [but] makes the problem worse for... reasons that should be entirely common sense." He then goes on to talk about the statistics behind the practice, the number of black people living in the UK, against the crime committed. There "are roughly 0.5% [of black people], that...actually kill somebody, and if you look at the police's own reports, they understand very well the type of boys [that] are likely to kill people are not random at all, when you adjust for abuse in the home, when you adjust for expulsion from school, crucially you start to see... the same socioeconomic demographic as the kids who have been doing this in Glasgow, or Liverpool, or Sheffield, in the 1920s, or Middlesbrough, but we can ignore all of that. So ironically treating the [remaining] % of young black boys in Hackney, who just want to go to school and get a job, like criminals, actually prevents us allocating the resources where they need to go, which is helping the most vulnerable people. The worst part about it, is if you're a kid...for example and you live on a council estate in Hackney...and you've been robbed two or three times growing up, you know boys have pulled a knife out, and took your mobile phone. Then you get searched [by] the police because of the very boys you're being bullied by, of course you're going to be p'd off, it's natural." (Akala, 2018)

Akala goes on to expand on the "lunacy of ethnically targeted stop and search further" and says "let's put it like this if we took the case of Jimmy Savile or Rolf Harris and said right, all white males in TV are potential pedophiles, and let's police Andrew Neil on the assumption when he goes to pick up his grandkids, let's just stop and make sure that they're his grandkids just in case, because of what Jimmy Savile done, this is what you get when you get collective blame, but we sort of accept it." He goes on to say he does not blame the public for this, but this is what happens as a result of public policy, "when you have a language of media that emphasizes race whenever there is a negative story... but not when there's a positive story". (Akala, 2018)

So we all live with this distortion of history and the narratives that emulate from this distortion, which allocates value and esteem according to where a person fits in relation to this narrative, regardless of whether or not they personally internally feel this way.

When writing on 'If History Is White' Dr Francis E. Kendall says: "The privilege of writing and teaching history only from the perspective of the colonizer, has such profound implications that they are difficult to fathom. As white people, we carry the stories we were taught as the truths, often failing to question those truths and discrediting those who do. There are many embedded privileges here:

- We are able to live in the absence of historical context. It is as if we are not forgetting our history, but acting as if it never happened. Or, if it did, it has nothing to do with us today
- ...We are taught that we are the only ones in the picture. If there were others, they obviously weren't worth mentioning.
- ...We are able to grow up without our racial supremacy's being questioned. It is so taken for

granted, such a foundation of all that we know, that we are able to be unconscious of it even though it permeates every aspect of our lives.

- ...We are taught little complicated history to have to sort through, think about, question, and so we have few opportunities to learn to grapple with complexities. We end up with simplistic sentiments...because we have only been taught fragments of information.

- ...We have the privilege of determining how and if historical characters and events will be remembered...we retain an extremely tight hold on what is and is not admitted and how information is presented. We do this as a culture, and we do it as individuals.

- ...We control what others know about their own histories by presenting only parts of a story. Because we all go to the same schools, if you will, everyone, regardless of color, is told the 'white' story." (Kendall, 2002)

We have a filtered history, which is being taught to the masses, with hugely powerful implications. We have a history that creates narratives and elevates some, whilst demonising others. We have a filtered history, which omits a vast amount of actual content.

In the chapter on 'The Press, the Messages Continue', I will elaborate, from research, just how much this version of history told, impacts on the psyche and culture of the nation.

TRAUMA

Trauma

The more I learn on this journey, the more I see there is much trauma out there. Everyone has their respective issues to deal with. We choose partners that match our attachment styles, whether helpful or not. We operate out of our patterns. Children come along, and they are further affected, whether that is for good or bad, by our attachment and parenting styles.

In my counselling training, one of the books I found the most fascinating, was the book Primal Wound, by Firman and Gila, which I alluded to earlier, in exploring the workshop for professionals with addictions. In the book, they explore a collective primal wound that sits underneath us, which is caused by 'non-being'.

'Non-being' in their book, is the experience of feeling underlying emotions such as guilt, shame, abandonment, feeling unloved, humiliated, powerless (for example), where the very existence of 'self-hood' is threatened. With this threat to 'self-hood', this threat of 'extinction' of self-hood, comes the threat of 'non-being', (non-existence of self-hood). The experience of 'Non-being' can be captured, in many ways, for example in some attachment styles, mentioned at the beginning of this book. The sense of 'non-being' (threat to self-hood) can also be triggered by not having needs met (hierarchy of needs) or experiencing racial and social perspectives that place you in an inferior position.

In their book, they explore the evolution of parenting and the ensuing trauma that has travelled down the centuries, such as the:

1. Infanticidal Mode (4th century) infanticide and sodomising of children

2. Abandonment Mode (4th to 13th century) physical and emotional abandonment

3. Ambivalent Mode (4th to 17th century) children were seen to be beaten into shape

4. Intrusive Mode (8th century) empathy began to appear/ dominating the mind and will of the child

5. Socialisation Mode (19th –mid 20th century) move from dominating to socialisation – Freud "channelling of the impulses."

6. Helping Mode (20th century) fully involves both parents in child's life/ as they work to empathise and fulfil its expanding needs.

"The historical overview leaves a trail of murder, abandonment and abuse......Thus the primal wound seems to inhere in a broad river of abuse and neglect, – often quite hidden as normal parenting practices/ normal cultural beliefs. At this level the primal wound is a universal wound in our collective spirit.... (although the book does not hinge on this broad evolutionary perspective)". (Firman F, 1997) However, the historical overview is important to note in the context of intergenerational trauma/ epigenetics, – where a traumatic experience is passed down through the generations.

The experience of Dehumanisation (non-being) is traumatic. There are many groups who have fought against this over the years, "such as the women's movement, the men's movement, the gay and lesbian movement, or the civil rights movement, all of which are devoted to the struggle against dehumanizing elements in our culture" (Firman F, 1997)

Trauma From Systemic And Structural Racism

In addition to the trauma that has travelled down the centuries, which many of us have experienced; if you are currently living in the UK, US and many cultures around the world, there can also be the hugely impactful trauma of racism. "Psychological distress is very much a part of everyday life for the child of color who is isolated, denigrated and mentally tortured. It is very much a part of life for the adolescent who is exhausted at the thought of dealing with another racist incident where s/he is forced to feel like an outsider, trapped under a spotlight that allows everyone to see and know what s/he really is. It is very much a part of life for the racialized adult who wakes up every morning to a reflection that is the 'wrong' color - a re-flection that will inevitably cause her/him to know pain, humiliation and fear." (George J. Sefa Dei, 2004)

If only you knew the pain and trauma that is faced in living as a black person in the UK. The dichotomy of facing different emotions. For example, many of us know that you can feel immense pain, for instance in losing a loved one, which countless of us have experienced.

There will be some point during the grieving process, however, whether that be in the short term, or long term, that something might happen, which makes you laugh. Does laughing cancel out the grief? No, the grief is very much still there.

For example, I lost an aunt in 2019; her death was very sudden. It was the strangest thing in the sense that on the day of her death, many of us had randomly taken time off work, or were at home for some reason. There were divisions in the family at the time, but her death had a way of reuniting everyone. We all rushed to hospital, and prayers were being said that she would live.

Unfortunately, she passed away. After she passed, we were invited into the room to see her. There were 20 of us in the room. I had unfortunately experienced the loss of loved ones before, but this was something I had never seen, for so many people to be at a person's bedside.

Where there were fractures, we all ended up, 20 of us, holding hands in a big circle around her bedside. We then returned to the family room. The Chaplin came along and said she must have been a very special woman? He said normally when he goes to bedsides, it is one or 2 people present. We agreed with him that she was special.

We wanted to give her a big send-off and celebration; this seemed to develop organically. After she passed stories seemed to emerge, where she was quietly supporting someone, caring for someone, helping someone. There were all of these stories that emerged and came together. Her funeral was huge as lots of people wanted to attend to pay their respects.

At her funeral, we had a DJ playing reflective music as we ate, with a microphone, as we wanted to have a time where people could share thoughts in her honour, if they felt inspired to do so. However, in the evening, the DJ played some more up-tempo music, from our playlist, and although people were so impacted by her loss, what did we do? Unusually, we danced. It was a dance of celebrating her life, a dance of celebrating life. We were in pain at her passing, but we danced and laughed together.

So, there you have the dichotomy, which I am sure many can relate to, the paradox of feeling pain, but still being able to dance and to laugh.

Which brings me onto my next point. As a person, you can have a good time within a painful environment. You can still sing, whilst mourning. You can sing to express your mourning.

There will be those BAME people in the UK, who make it to senior managers, CEO's, DR's, entrepreneurs etc. Implicit bias and racism are painful and can be internalized, so there will be those that attempt not to see, or bury the fact that they have seen, and get on with life.

However, there are many for whom the pain and trauma of living in the UK as a BAME person is so present. You have no idea of the pain. And no, I am not talking about the ordinary dynamic of 'we all go through pleasure and pain', – I am talking about an experience, so impactful, so oppressive, so painful, because of the colour of your skin, – in this country, – in the UK!

As part of writing, although I know these dynamics experientially, and feel they are so intrinsic to my experience of living in the UK, and a shared understanding by others who experience it, I didn't want the experiences captured to be just mine. I wanted to look at research, and I wanted to hear from others to pull out some of the themes that BAME people experience, living in the UK? So, as mentioned, I did some focus Groups with BAME professionals

One of the themes that emerged from the findings was from supporting and seeing other black professionals, that had reached senior positions in the public service, being unfairly disciplined in the workplace and seeing some of these professionals, having breakdowns, and ending up in the mental health system.

There was the huge emotional impact of seeing and supporting these people, being left feeling 'like a quivering wreck', and also being left with the unsettling thought of 'there but for the grace of God, go I'.

These breakdowns ensued from the treatment they experienced in institutions where there was institutional racism. If these occurrences seem alien, to gain a little understanding of this dynamic, think of the Shilpa Shetty, Big Brother experience, which was televised on our TV screens in 2007.

At the time, the treatment of Shilpa Shetty caused international outrage and debates about whether there was racism in the UK. I have to say that watching the dynamic of treatment played out towards Shilpa Shetty, was not unfamiliar and not unfamiliar with other BAME people I had discussions with at the time! I am always really struck when there are debates of racism, that the people who *could* never, and *would* never experience it, become the experts in deciding whether or not it is happening!

A few years ago, I put together a workshop for BAME women. The workshop was prompted by my cousin's dissertations some years earlier, for which she ran a series of focus groups for BAME women to look at their experiences in the workplace, as she was seeking to understand these, understand organisational change and steps that support career progression. She ran a series of focus groups to interview women and ascertain their experiences. She asked me to help her type up the recordings.

In typing up the recordings, I could hear alarming common themes, that sounded painful. It was this that prompted me to arrange the workshop, to have a forum which supported these women. The themes that emerged were being 'left out' in some way, finding that in organisations decisions are made in social settings, and missing out on these networks and decision-making processes, in being left out.

I was so moved at the time by the common themes that were presenting themselves from these focus groups, that I organised a conference, with my cousin, to put thoughts together to see what we could do to support BAME women, and address some of the issues that emerged from hearing about their experiences in the UK workplace. One woman, in particular, fed back, almost ten years later, that the workshop was life-changing for her. I think it was the element of having a supportive space, which helped her at the time.

Another issue which surfaced in the recent focus groups I held was about the impact of migration on African & Afro Caribbean communities. Migration caused issues of childhood separation and childhood trauma, which 'leads to intergenerational trauma (potentially)'. Attachment is a subject I mentioned at the beginning of my book, which obviously affects all communities. In exploring the themes of this book, implicit bias and the array of strands connected to this, as mentioned previously, attachment was an emerging theme. Due to the impact of people coming to the UK, and leaving their children behind, or the trend of some West Africans to foster their children into white families, there are related attachment issues which affect the BAME community. In the focus group it was expressed how difficult it has been in repairing relationships with parents and siblings, from the experience of separation and living with the ramifications and implications of this.

Trauma and its many expressions, and its impact on health, was a theme which repeatedly emerged in the focus groups. Also, intergenerational trauma, which it was felt influenced our behaviours, but "doesn't excuse what we have to go against on a day to day basis."

There was the sense that we don't seem to access talking therapies much. That we live with our stresses & our traumas, and they influence and impact us in a way that sometimes can be very detrimental. The fact of having the external pressures of the world we live in, the way unconscious bias and discrimination operates, not having our strengths recognized, and then not processing this in a way that enables us and helps us get the best for ourselves in this world.

I looked at some interesting research on the Psychological Trauma connected to race and ethnicity, which stated: "Previous scholars have hypothesized that the cumulative impact of these three diverse types of racism - overt racism, systemic and structural racism, and racial microaggressions - can result in trauma, otherwise known as racial trauma. (Bryant-Davis, 2007; Bryant-Davis & Ocampo, 2006, Comas-Díaz, 2016). When people of color experience trauma related to race or ethnicity, they are more likely to undergo behavioral or personality related changes that are often pervasive and long-lasting and align with typical symptoms of Post-Traumatic Stress Disorder (PTSD); Carter & Sant-Barker, 2015). People who struggle with pervasive and painful experiences with racism are encouraged to reframe their perspectives or to 'get over it', instead of being validated that they are experiencing 'normal' and 'expected' responses to trauma." (Nadal, 2019)

The research talks about the fact that when experiencing the trauma of racism, it is not easy to simply walk away or step out of the trauma source, which could be at work, through laws, policies or in public spaces. Therefore, people facing the trauma of racism are constantly retraumatized.

"Because people of color experience microaggressions regularly in their lives, they may have an array of emotional, cognitive, and psychological reactions that often lead to psychological and physical health consequences (Sue, 2010; Torino et al., 2019). However, when microaggressions are so pervasive (i.e., they are experienced with high intensity), they significantly impair a person's daily functioning, may cause significant psychological distress, and may activate or exacerbate typical PTSD symptoms – including, but not limited to – hypervigilance, anxiety, avoidant behavior, and intrusive thoughts) … Given the results which indicated that racial microaggressions that occur in the workplace or school settings are significantly associated with trauma, it is critical to understand how microaggression that occurs in settings of places of learning or employment can be detrimental and potentially traumatizing.…So, while racial microaggressions may appear innocuous or harmless, they may trigger memories of intensity or frequent racial discrimination, which may exacerbate trauma symptoms." (Nadal, 2019)

To think about some practical examples of how these systemic and structural scenarios play out, which "may have an array of emotional, cognitive, and psychological reactions that often lead to psychological and physical health consequences (Sue, 2010; Torino et al., 2019)". We live in an inequitable world. You start out in the world, very much expecting the same for everyone. You soon begin to learn that white people are treated differently than black people. They are treated differently by white people, by Asians and by blacks (as per the social construct of race). To navigate through, you have to build in strategies, learn the system, build in ways of interacting; you have to build in resilience.

In the film 'Becoming', Michelle Obama talks about her upbringing. She said, "our dinner table was the first table where I felt like I belonged, and then you go out into the world expecting the same thing." She then discusses being in high school, accomplished, a senior class treasurer, on the honour roll, and went to see her guidance counsellor about her aspiration to go to Princeton. However, her guidance counsellor decided that her wish to go to Princeton was thinking too big; she was reaching too high and that "she did not think that Michelle was Princeton material". (Becoming, 2020)

Thankfully, we know that Michelle did become very successful, however, she says in the 'Becoming' video, that whilst she was able to get over the statement, "it was a punch". (Becoming, 2020)

In terms also of exploring the dynamic of race in the UK, I think of the recent experience of Belly Mujinga. Belly was a journalist, yet in the UK she was working in a ticket office in Victoria. Whilst there is obviously nothing wrong with working in a ticket office in Victoria, my comment is prompted by my experience and observation that Belly would not be 'journalist material' in the UK.

Reggie Yates, TV presenter, Radio DJ and actor commented in a 2016 interview that "I'm very aware of my heritage, that I'm a young black man and that there are no other young black men like me on the telly," (Standard, 2016)

An article in the Independent entitled 'Who'd be a traffic warden?' noted the demographic of 75 wardens working in South London. "90 per cent of them are Africans and half of those are graduates." The attendant the journalist accompanied was 'a computer science graduate from Nigeria'. He "has worked as an attendant for three years. He says his degree is not recognised in this country and explains that his position isn't unique: one of his former supervisors was a qualified radiographer...Most have been either kicked, punched or spat at during their rounds. All are abused, virtually on a daily basis." (Independent, 2006)

My observation of life experience in the UK, is that many institutions in the City and Canary Wharf, as per the hierarchy of race, have BAME staff working as cleaners, caterers, and service staff, and white males in the Boardrooms. This is the implicit model of operation that goes unnoticed, unnoted and remains intrinsic and 'completely comfortable'.

Belly articulated to her employees that she had vulnerabilities and health issues, but they were not considered, and she was moved onto the concourse to work during the COVID-19 pandemic. Whilst she was on the concourse, a 'smartly dressed man' "approached her and asked, 'Why are you here?' She told him, 'Can't you see my uniform? I'm working here.' He told her, 'I have coronavirus and I'm giving it to you,' and spat at her." (Journalists, 2020)

As in keeping, although this situation was unfair, horrific, unjust and had the ultimate consequence for Belly, let alone the unimaginable impact on her husband and daughter, there was no systemic recompense.

There were absolutely no repercussions for the 'smartly dressed man' who spat on her, yet walked away 'unsullied' by his actions. In fact, I would say he was systemically protected from his actions, as I don't recall his name ever being mentioned.

The British Transport Police carried out an investigation and "took no further action in the case because they did not find CCTV evidence that she had been spat at or coughed on." (Guardian, 2020). Her employer "Southern Railway, said it followed all of the latest Government health advice"! (Standard, 2020)

Adrian Durham did a brilliant, passionate talk on TalkSport to address those who respond to the slogan of 'Black Lives Matter' with saying 'All Lives Matter'. In his talk, he says before working at TalkSport, he "was a news reporter and covered two famous murder cases. One was the stabbing to death of Phillip Lawrence, a Headmaster at a London school, who was white, well respected and a father of 4. Less than a year after his stabbing, the murderer was convicted at the Old Bailey. The other murder case was that of Stephen Lawrence, a teenage black boy from London, stabbed to death by racists at a bus stop in 1993. Police were given the suspects names a day after the murder. Four years after the murder, a National newspaper named the people they believed killed Stephen. Five years after the murder, police apologized to the family for failures in the investigation. Six years after, the met police were accused of institutionalised racism and incompetence. Nineteen years later, 2 of the men on the original list of suspects, were found guilty of murder and sentenced to life." (Durham, 2020)

You see these are the types of systemic and structural inequalities we are challenged with. The "cumulative impact of these three diverse types of racism - overt racism, systemic and structural racism, and racial microaggressions, ... - can result in trauma, otherwise known as racial trauma." (Bryant-Davis, 2007; Bryant-Davis & Ocampo, 2006, Comas-Díaz, 2016).

This is the pain of the experience in the UK, which then manifests in all sorts of health issues. If you try to connect these everyday experiences to race, people get upset. In her book White Fragility, which I always recommend people read, Robin Di Angelo says: "suggesting that white people have racial prejudice is perceived as saying that we are bad and should be ashamed. We then feel the need to defend our character, rather than explore the inevitable racial prejudices we have absorbed so that we might change them.".... "Given how seldom we experience racial discomfort in a society we dominate, we haven't had to build our racial stamina. Socialized into a deeply internalized sense of superiority that we are either unaware of or can never admit to ourselves, we become highly fragile in conversations about race. We consider a challenge to our racial worldviews as a challenge to our very identity's as good moral people. Thus, we perceive any attempt to connect us to the system of racism as an unsettling and unfair moral offence. The smallest amount of racial stress is intolerable." (DiAngelo, 2019)

She also writes "when a racial groups collective prejudice is backed by the power of legal authority and institutional control, it is transformed into racism, a far-reach system that functions independently from the intention or self-images of individual actors." (DiAngelo, 2019)

I recall an experience I had at the age of 15 or so, whilst shopping with my mum. We lived in Fulham at the time and had gone shopping in Shepherds Bush market.

We walked into a large convenience store, and I trailed behind my mum as she picked up items and put them in the basket. At one point, I remember looking at one of the men who worked in the shop and I semi-smiled, as I wasn't sure of his expression looking at me. However, when we got to the tills, the man accused me of stealing something!! His words were he 'saw' me take something.

I was so shocked that he had said that and began to defend myself. He wanted me to empty my pockets. I said I would not empty my pockets, as I knew I had not stolen anything.

My mum was confident that I had not stolen anything and said, "go on Suzann, empty your pockets and show him." I proceeded to empty my pockets, and out came the tissues, the coins, etc., until the linings were unturned. There were no stolen items in my pockets!

My mum was enraged. She gave the man a piece of her mind and left the basket full of contents, on the shop counter. I remember the confusion I felt, in knowing I was innocent, and I had not done anything!! I could not understand why the man had accused me. The shock of simply going about your day and having someone randomly accuse you of something that you know you had no connection to doing.

Imagine the feelings of black men, who are stopped by police constantly, whilst driving, whilst walking, at times surrounded by multiple policemen, whilst society goes by staring, on cars and buses, viewing the scene as 'normal'. Imagine the impact on psyche, knowing, in many cases, they are innocent. In his interview with James O'Brien Akala talks of being stopped by police on his way to the Royal Institution of Mathematics Masterclasses, he says this is when it hit him "respectability politics don't mean anything. Because I was born in the bottom 1 or 2 % socioeconomically speaking, academically I was in the top 1 or 2%, it didn't change the fact that some of the people with the power just saw a criminal." (Akala, 2018)

I recently read some disturbing facts about being 'exonerated'. "Exoneration occurs when the conviction for a crime is reversed, either through demonstration of innocence, a flaw in the conviction, or otherwise". (Wikipedia, 2010) A report in 2017 showed that although African American's are only 13% of the US population, they accounted for 1,900 exonerations. On top of this there were 15 large scale police scandals where a further 1800 innocent men were exonerated! The reasons given for these disproportionate figures are that "police enforce drug laws more vigorously against African Americans than against members of the white majority, despite strong evidence that both groups use drugs at equivalent rates. African Americans are more frequently stopped, searched, arrested, and convicted —including in cases in which they are innocent. The extreme form of this practice is systematic racial profiling in drug-law enforcement." (Gross, et al., 2017)

Alfred Chestnut, Ransom Watkins and Andrew Steward (African Americans) were teenagers when they were sentenced to life in prison in 1984, for a crime they did not commit. They were exonerated of murder in 2019, after spending 36 years in prison. (Post, 2019). There are other stories that come to mind such as the central park 5, African American children, who were framed for an attack they did not commit, on a central park white jogger.

Imagine the impact on psyche, the pain, trauma, anger, feeling of injustice, emotional distress from being sentenced for a crime you *know* you have not committed. Imagine how disturbing it must feel not to be heard, not to be listened to, knowing you are innocent. Let alone the impact to your life, your loss of freedom, loss of plans, disconnection from your family and relationships, all when knowing you are innocent. The impact on 'self' and the sprawling impact on members of your family.

Dr Carl C. Bell and Edward Dunbar, so aptly and powerfully describe the mental tussle that takes place, in navigating systemic inequality and describes racism 'as being akin to torture and terrorism' (Pierce 1982). Their paper talks about the psychological navigation in trying to figure out which white people generally like you, and which ones are tolerating you and that "[r]ejecting the former, is as great an error as trusting the latter" (Bell, 2013). They also reference amygdala responses when people look at black faces (touched on in the chapter on how we operate out of unconscious information). They talk about the destructive actions of systemic functions when a BAME person] "is truly accepted by a white person and, consequently, erroneously begins to believe that racism no longer exists." (Bell, 2013)

We all, regardless of race, face our respective circumstances which we have to navigate through, whether that be relational, familial, educational, financial, issues of health, sexuality, gender, religion or other dynamics. All of this is important and not always particularly easy. On top of this, we are all working within the biased corporate messaging and 'Public Relations', which is fed through the lens of history, media, film, TV and which either promotes or demonises, according to where you fit in the hierarchy of race. We know that advertising works, having repeated messages about a product, which then influences choices. Companies invest numerous amounts of money on this premise. In 2019 "it was estimated advertising spending worldwide [would] surpass 560 billion U.S. dollars." (Statista, 2020)

Intergenerational Trauma For Descendants Of Slaves And Slave Owners

In considering trauma and researching for this book, themes that kept emerging were 'disavowal', 'denial' and 'shame'.

On writing this book, I referred to the shared history of slavery, as 'A Difficult Past', as I know as a therapist how challenging it can be to look at uncomfortable information. I know how much easier it is to stay in a place "to know and not know." (Hall, 2013)

As a counsellor, (as well as from personal and life experience), I am aware of what is called (John Bradshaw's 1988 term) the 'family trance'. (Firman F, 1997). The family trance has its roots in the family of origin and demands from us "compliance rather than authenticity, [and demands] conformity rather than free will." (Firman F, 1997)

Within the 'family trance', we assume roles and the 'family trance' demands and requires that we stay within those roles. These assumed roles are not necessarily about authenticity but fitting into the family narrative.

For instance, you can be in a family structure and love your family, but feel pain at certain dynamics, or even witness unpleasant dynamics, but push aside these feelings or events. This can happen because of love for the family structure. Or this can happen because of not wanting to lose or threaten the familiarity, and 'security' of the structure.

It takes huge journeying and courage sometimes to admit how dynamics have made you feel. It can take a tremendous amount of processing to accept the pain that you feel may have been caused by family. It can cause feelings of guilt, feelings of betrayal, it is easier to accept the family trance and narrative that ensues. For instance, I know in deep conversations with long term friends, it has taken years for them to talk about or hold a particular family dynamic, which really hurt or affected them. Even in acknowledging these feelings, there is guilt for feeling you might be accusing someone.

I shared at the beginning of this book that I had an MS scare, where I had lost sight in one eye. As shared previously, this was a wake-up call for me! I knew there was a situation in my life, with which I had been really open about with my friends, but had never been open about with family. In keeping with the 'family trance' which is hugely powerful, I was staying with the family identity, staying within the family's assigned role.

We are a large gregarious family, whom everyone loves on meeting us as a group. However, I knew I had experienced and was a survivor of sexual abuse, and I felt holding onto this 'secret' was impacting my health.

I would always look at a cousin of mine who had come out as gay years before, and I loved his courage, I loved that he was living a life that was authentic to him. I felt I wasn't living an authentic life, as there was always this huge 'secret' that I was carrying.

With the MS scare, involving loss of eyesight in one eye, which thankfully was temporary, I wrote a letter of disclosure to my family, to share with them about the abuse.

Well, that went down well! Not! As can happen with disclosure of sexual abuse, there was huge fall-out, 'victim-blaming', the breakdown of some relationships as well as support from other members. "Confrontations and disclosures can be difficult, frightening, painful and demanding. Yet they are also opportunities to express your feelings directly, to break the twisted part of secrecy, to assert your own needs and boundaries, to overcome your fears, and to act for yourself. All these are potent steps in working through the victimisation of abuse. Whatever the consequences, it's common to feel some sense of relief mixed in with your other emotions. There is no longer a secret in the air. There is no longer hiding." (Davis, 1988)

I have to say, although the journey was difficult, the sense of freedom that came from no longer carrying such a secret and living an authentic life, was liberating.

At the end of my level 3 counselling training, I did a presentation on the impact of child sexual abuse, obviously as it's a subject close to my heart. I did some research at the time and explored a report done by the NSPCC called 'No one noticed, no one heard'. The report was a study of disclosure of childhood abuse where they interviewed 60 young adults aged 18-24 years.

"The young adults were asked whether they had tried to tell anyone about what was happening to them, and what had happened as a result of their disclosures. Although much research suggests that few children disclose sexual abuse, in this study over 80% had tried to tell someone about the abuse." (Allnock, 2013)

The evidence in the report was just as the title described, that 'No one noticed, no one heard'. There was the heartbreaking experience of children who longed for someone to see what was happening to them, who longed for someone to help them and to see the signs. It was totally heart-rending to read, especially as I so identified, and made me wonder at the time, how many children are out there, in this situation, just longing for someone to notice? The signs are always there! However, I know my thoughts on this are for a separate conversation/ piece of writing.

I know with my own experience, I spent decades living within the family trance! I know the conflict of what it is to "know and not know." (Hall, 2013) I know how it is to live with elephants in the room, and even though metaphorically the elephants are releasing dung, and the atmosphere is smelly and uncomfortable, everyone steps over and simply makes a cup of tea.

Such is the power of knowing, but not knowing. You stay within the safety of the existing structure. You stay within all that is known. You do not desire to encounter what is beyond the fear of the unknown.

In considering what it is "to know and not know." (Hall, 2013) and repeated themes that kept on emerging in researching for this book, such as 'disavowal', 'denial' and 'shame', I continued researching further. I am very aware from life experience and counselling training that things that we push away and wish not to look at, do not disappear; they remain. The things that we deny, simply manifest in different ways, they find a voice of expression.

I wondered, in suppressing the shared history of slavery and empire, what is the impact of this on psyche and trauma on all involved? How can such a hugely traumatic past, with suffering and violence witnessed by the victims and perpetrators be simply neatly packed away? We are aware of war veterans experiencing Post Traumatic Stress Disorder (PTSD). "...witnessing or experiencing a traumatic event is described as the source of PTSD symptoms. PTSD may be caused by combat, abuse, emotional loss, terrorist attacks, natural disasters, serious accidents, assault, and many other situations." (Benefits, 2020)

My research in trying to understand the trauma aspect of slavery on all, led me back to attachment theory, which I had written about at the beginning of this book, and how violence and anger was modelled. The "'Master slave relationship became the template for all human relationships whether within a marriage between parent and child or between employer and employee' (Gump, 2010, p. 47.)" Thomas Jefferson showed his understanding "'of the consequences of slavery that bequeath generations of physical and psychological suffering to America's future black citizenry, while it doomed America's white progeny to becoming the custodians of an invasive and pernicious racism'" (Leary, 2005, p. 218.)" (Gilda, 2014)

Jefferson is quoted as follows: "There must be doubtless an unhappy influence on the manners of our people produced by the existence of slavery among us. The whole commerce between master and slave is a perpetual exercise of the most boisterous passions, the most unrelenting despotism on the one part, and degrading submission on the other part. Our children see this, and learn to imitate it; for man is an imitative animal...And with what execration should the statesman be loaded, who permitting one half of the citizens thus to trample on the rights of others, transforms those into despots, and these into enemies, destroys the morals of the one part, and the amor patriae [love of country] of the other...(Leary 2005, pp. 218-219)." (Gilda, 2014)

The same research looks at, as a consequence of the master slave relationship template the "transmission of shame through the generations by way of unempathic parenting... [leading] to an attachment style that is classified as 'insecure'. Graph, 2011." (Gilda, 2014)

At the beginning of this book, I talked about attachment theory and mentioned four types: (1): Secure; (2): Avoidant; (3): Ambivalent and (4): Disorganised. An "Insecure" attachment style would include the (2): Avoidant attachment style (Insecure Avoidant) and the (3): Ambivalent attachment style (Insecure Ambivalent/ Resistant) under its umbrella.

To recap on this, there are a range of likely outcomes, of how these attachment styles affect a person relating in the world. For example a person who may have experienced an '**Avoidant**' attachment style, (Insecure Avoidant), where the mother was dismissive, critical, irritable, distant, etc., might feel rejected or isolated in life. They may also have a tendency to feel stressed and scared. For someone who has experienced the '**Ambivalent**' attachment style, (Insecure Ambivalent/ Resistant), where a mother may have been inconsistent, indifferent and insensitive, they might feel stressed and insecure, angry and susceptible to feeling emotional abandonment. They may be unsociable and aggressive.

So, if according to research, shame is passed through the generations, leading to an attachment style that is classified as "insecure as a consequence of the master-slave relationship" which "became the template for all human relationships" (Gump,

2010, p. 47.), there will be many people who have experienced these insecure attachment styles. People who have experienced these types of attachment styles have felt "rejection rather than acceptance" and "control rather than cooperation". (Gilda, 2014) The research talks about how these styles continue across the generations. "Insecure individuals, who have grown up with rejecting, unpredictable and/or frightening parents, adopt a "defensive narrowing of attention in order to deal with the problem, ...of knowing what you are not supposed to know and feeling what you are not supposed to feel... And so it goes from generation to generation!" (Gilda, 2014)

As with anything, however, these attachments styles do not need to be the end of the story! Someone who has had an Insecure (Ambivalent or Avoidant) or Disorganised attachment style, can heal from the experience. Having healthy relationships, having healthy external mirrors, healing, including talking therapies, can change the effects of the attachment style and break the intergenerational chain of this type of trauma.

In terms of the relational template of slavery, which would be mirrored by those who observed, and has impacted attachment styles, which are passed down the generations, it led me to consider and research on the "long-established British and colonial preparatory and public boarding school tradition...[In] government most of the policymakers are ex-boarders. They are also represented in all of the major institutions in Britain." (Schaverien, 2015)

The research I looked at shows that although some people have positive experiences of the boarding school structure, they are a minority. Research talks of the psychological trauma experienced by early boarders and the ensuing conflicting emotions in knowing they are from 'privileged' backgrounds, so should not complain; the impact of knowing that their parents have chosen and paid for this life for them and the 'cultural amnesia' that accompanies managing the [repressed] trauma and conflicting emotions [from events experienced]. (Schaverien, 2015)

So, we see further evidence of the shared history of slavery and colonialism, impacting the present and fostering trauma.

Following on from the intergenerational attachment impact, there is the consideration of the intergenerational impact of 'Posttraumatic Slave Syndrome' (PTSS), and its impact on the Patriarchal Nuclear Family Structure (PNFS). "Refusal to remember, denial, dissociation, and disavow are all echoed in the absence of slavery from the trauma literature and, until recently, from psychoanalytic literature. Trauma literature gives attention to the Holocaust, floods, earthquakes, sexual abuse, rape, etc. but not to slavery. Only recently has psychoanalysis turned any attention to slavery and racism." (Gilda, 2014)

However, a conceptual framework was developed by Dr Joy De-Gruy, exploring the multigenerational impact of adaptive behaviour to slavery and oppression, which is often undiagnosed and leads to PTSD or specifically 'Post Traumatic Slave Syndrome' (PTSS).

Research looking at the impact of trauma on the Patriarchal Nuclear family structure and African American male to female relationships, is based on US statistics, however, the threads and themes (as with bias and racism generally) are relevant to the UK. The research says that although African male to female relationships are resilient, "forced adaptations to structural racism in the United States may have resulted in some attitudes and behaviors that undermine the development of healthy relationships... (DeGruy, 2005; Edin & Kefalas, 2005). The discrepancy between the desire to achieve the patriarchal nuclear family structure (PNFS) in the United States and experiences of structural racism is at the crux of understanding adverse relationship outcomes among African American men and women (Franklin, 2000)." (Noelle M. St. Vil, 2019)

"The trauma-informed perspective recognizes the prevalence

and impact of trauma in the lives of people (Harris & Fallot, 2001; Levenson, 2017). When people experience trauma, they adapt to survive. The adaption to trauma and the various ways trauma manifests itself is normal. However, the adapted attitudes and behaviors may be unhealthy to successful functioning in daily life (Harris & Fallot, 2001; Levenson, 2017)."... "PTSS [posttraumatic slave syndrome] is a concept developed by Dr Joy DeGruy (2005) to illustrate the adverse effects of institutionalized racism in the lives of African Americans." (Noelle M. St. Vil, 2019)

The research goes on to talk about the effects of African Americans being treated as 'property' of white people for 246 years during slavery. Their marriages were not seen as legal during this time and "were undermined, violated and traumatized." (Noelle M. St. Vil, 2019) They talk through processes (such as convict leasing) which "signals the beginning of the prison industrial complex and the disproportionate incarceration of masses of African American men (Fierce, 1994), leaving many African American families without husbands and fathers to be the heads of households." (Noelle M. St. Vil, 2019)

The research talks about the "incarceration rate of African American men, who account for only 6 per cent of the general population but represent nearly 50 per cent of the prison population (Perry & Bright, 2012)." (Noelle M. St. Vil, 2019) In terms of the prison statistics in the UK, a report published by the Ministry of Justice Analytical Services states: "black people are almost four times more likely than white people in Britain to be in prison." At the start of their report, it says: "The landscape of disproportionality for black, Asian and minority ethnic (BAME) individuals in the criminal justice system (CJS) is complex." (Noah Uhrig, 2016) "Despite making up just 14% of the population, BAME men and women make up 25% of prisoners, while over 40% of young people in custody are from BAME backgrounds." (Lammy, 2017)

The research looks at the significant impact of structural racism and PTSS on African Americans, the adaptive behaviours that ensue in trying to navigate through structural racism. There is a consequential impact on relationships and the impact on the Patriarchal Family Structure. There is almost a double whammy impact from this. Although there are thriving black marriages, there is (1): the *actual* impact from structural racism on relationships; (2): the *perception* and *portrayal* of black families and fathers, without consideration of the destructive influence of slavery and systemic racism.

The report also talks about the impact on relationships due to men facing socioeconomic disadvantage and being blocked from opportunities; anger felt due to barriers created by systemic racism and oppression and 'racial socialization'.

'Ghosts' are a repeated theme that emerged in researching intergenerational trauma as a consequence of slavery on all, as in psychological ghosts. The effects of suppressed information, which simply gets expressed in other ways, was a repeated theme. Denial, disavowal and disassociation do not make events and their aftermath go away. "Traumatic events are not isolated occurrences, and the inner experience of the traumatized individual becomes reflected in the wider world...Traumatic reactions spill over from the individual to the collective in parallel processes which maintain and reinforce the trauma (Soth 2007:74)." (Taylor, 2014)

In keeping with the theme of Ghosts and the effects of unspoken trauma, there has been work by Professor Maurice Apprey, which theorizes the 'Transgenerational Haunting' in African American communities. He looks at how unspoken trauma appears in different forms in one generation to the next, such as suicide in one generation, murder in the next, and abuse in the following. This theme is in keeping with much research on trauma, that it cannot be contained or simply left, it will find an expression.

Aimé Césaire (French Poet) links the Holocaust to slavery and colonialism as a 'terrific boomerang effect'. "He argues that before the Europeans became the victims of Nazism they were accomplices, 'that they tolerated that Nazism before it was inflicted on them they absolved it they shut their eyes to it legitimised it because until then it had applied only to the non-European peoples.' (Schwab, 2010, p.47)" (Gilda, 2014)

The "genocide of indigenous people under the colonial and imperial rule was silenced in a defensive discourse of progressing civilization, but it returned with a vengeance. Race and bureaucracy were the two main devices used under fascism during the return to the heart of Europe of the violence against other human beings developed under colonial and Imperial rule. For Arendt, the ghosts of colonial and imperial violence propelled the Jewish Holocaust." (Schwab, 2010)

When looking at the collective impact of slavery, in addition to the above themes, other themes that emerged were feelings of shame, guilt and having a wound. Talking about race is an emotive subject and one subject where people can easily feel accused. In one Independent US study, looking at how white Americans remember and make meaning of slavery, one participant stated that society is "impacted greatly in terms of the national shame and guilt". Another participant stated: "I'm sure that in terms of a collective psyche, it's had a huge impact on white people and I think that's one of the reasons we have such a hard time talking, still talking about slavery and racism today, because it's such a wounded place, because how could we have let that kind of stuff go on and how do we continue to let it go on." (Parker, 2010)

The impact of slavery and colonialism has far-reaching consequences. There is the continued structural and systemic mode of operation and its effects on health, psyche, socio and economic disadvantage. There is also the accompanying denial, disavowal, and disassociation, which fuels the explosive impact of trauma (which cannot be contained). There is also PTSS, and the effect of the 'master-slave' relationship template, which has influenced attachment styles, and feelings of shame and guilt.

The recurring theme of 'ghosts' in trauma research indicates that the undealt with 'violent silent' pasts, or traumatic events, seem to keep emerging in different ways. Maybe the 'violent silent' pasts are calling for our attention so that we can eliminate the trauma from being passed on to future generations.

THE PRESS,
THE MESSAGES
CONTINUE

In the very early stages of counselling training, we touched on diversity. In introducing this subject, we went through a simple group exercise, where adjectives to describe people were displayed on the flipchart, such as American, Irish, Black, Mexican, etc. We were given a set time and the objective of the exercise was to write as many things that came to mind for each description. At the end of the exercise, as a group, we read out the lists that we had written down.

I remember being struck during that exercise, how much information I had inside of me concerning each of the descriptions. Just by seeing the name, I could access a vast amount of stored content attached to each title. I remember wondering where all of that information had come from. It was amazing how many commonalities we shared, in writing and how much we had categorized each title.

At this time, we were getting to know each other as a group, and nothing written down or shared to all was negative. In my mind, I queried whether as a group, we were being polite and whether there were negative associations, which had not been shared.

In the final years of counselling training, as shared at the beginning of this book, we really started to dig into issues of diversity. We started to dig into our differences and question, how do we really see the other and what comes up for us, in looking at the other? What are our fears, what are our triggers, it was a huge amount of exploration.

I learnt much from my peers during presentations of their self-reflections. For instance, one of our peers, (and I share this story with her permission) had faced a physically violent attack in the past. On our course, another of our peers looked just like the attacker, in terms of being from the same culture of the man who had attacked her. We were oblivious to this, as she had a very close relationship with this peer, and it was not until nearer the end of the course during her presentation, we learnt just how much she had to work through.

She had to work through all that emerged from seeing and meeting this peer. She had to process through the distress of what had happened to her, which she has now moved beyond. She had to process through and be honest about the triggers the connections to this peer brought up, whilst allowing this peer to be known for who he really was. It was letting this peer be known for who he really was, which caused them to have a strong friendship. However, this was enabled by her doing a lot of processing and could have instantly been derailed on meeting him and knowing what he represented to her.

Therein, we see the beauty of honesty in acknowledging what it is that you really feel and allowing yourself to process through this, so it does not become a barrier. "All humans have prejudice; we cannot avoid it. If I am aware that a social group exists, I will have gained information about that group from the society around me. This information helps me make sense of the group from my cultural framework. People who claim not to be prejudiced are demonstrating a profound lack of self-awareness." (DiAngelo, 2019)

Our tutors stressed how important it was for us to go through the process of self-awareness around diversity, to avoid difference and pre-conceived ideas informing the counselling sessions, and therefore inhibiting the client. In not acknowledging your lens on difference, in pushing it away, you are more likely to operate out of it. In processing through, you are more enabled to put it aside.

Implicit Social Representations - The Norm and 'The Other'

After Harry and Meghan left the UK, there was much robust debate about whether race did play a part in causing them to leave. Indeed, there was your own comment that "Meghan and Harry haven't been criticised because of her colour but because she's a selfish social climber and he's a weak whiner - and by playing this despicable race card they have grossly libelled all of Britain" (Mail, 2020)

I have to say; my observation is that I often feel with news reporting, it seems we are being encouraged and directed to make negative associations with specific races and specific religions. For example, linking knife crime to 'black' people. Or if religion is mentioned, it is usually to demonise and link to a crime, such as terrorism, e.g. 'Muslim terrorist'. The stories are reported in ways which cause us to attach negative connections to colour and crime, or religion and crime. However, these connections to colour and crime or religion and crime, are not encouraged if the subject is white. For instance, it would be unheard of to attach colour or religion in reporting on Jimmy Saville, Rolf Harris, and Mira Hindley, etc. In these instances, it would be deemed ludicrous or unnecessary to mention colour or religion.

However, in keeping with writing this book, I really wanted to seek to understand more about this dynamic. I wanted to know what the cogs are, that are part of the larger wheel and how everything fitted together. I wanted to explore whether racial bias in the media was substantiated or could be understood, so I began to research, and my research took me on a journey.

I came across research produced in Vienna, by the European Research Centre on Migration and Ethnic Relations. In their report, they state "it is assumed that racism is communicated through the media in the form of social representations. This means that the image of immigrants and the interpretation of ethnic relations in the media is not deliberately distorted and not by individuals, but rather that media are an influential part of a larger process of (re) production of social representations in the public sphere. Journalists and media institutions often reproduce forms of ethnic inequality 'by default'; i.e. they do not do so consciously, but inadvertently, for example as part of their professional routine and constraints inherent to news making. Racism in the media is often not blatant: it is precisely the implicit stereotypical representations, generalising or justifying statements, or even the very 'absence' of ethnic minorities' viewpoints in news about them, that produce the widespread prejudiced beliefs and the legitimisation of exclusionary practices and hostility towards them." ((ERCOMER), 2002)

I felt conflicted about their research, as I thought although much of this is implicit, it should not absolve any of us from personal responsibility, especially when you look at the macro effect from the messaging of inequality, particularly where it fosters scenarios like Amy Cooper, and also situations like George Floyd, where the black male has been so dehumanised.

In looking at the above research, I wanted to understand things further. I was already aware of the power of the implicit, from my counselling training and its forcefulness in influencing our actions. I was aware of the process of forming our self-concept and our concept of others. It was helpful to explore and learn more about our shared unspoken past and explore how this might impact on interactions. It was helpful also to explore and learn more about the hierarchy of race and the implicit implications of this. It was insightful to look further at trauma and its repercussions.

Prompted by the above paper, I therefore decided to do some exploration around 'social representations', to understand more about this dynamic of bias and the bigger picture that informs interactions.

My search led me to some hugely insightful research by the White Rose Consortium, of the Universities of Leeds, Sheffield and York. They published a paper in 2018, which explored the British Values curriculum policy in English Schools. Part of their approach was tracing the history of Britishness in the curriculum and analysing this using a psycho-political approach. I have tried to pull out the key themes of their report, (relevant to this writing) which I feel are educational and support an understanding of the macro picture of ingesting information, and how "the language of anti-racism can co-exist alongside racist beliefs and actions." (Mills, 2018)

The report states that: Following the Manchester and London terror attacks in 2017, the then UK Prime Minister, Theresa May announced the need to assert 'the superiority' of British Values into the school system. However, embedding 'Britishness' into the curriculum was hard to define as ..."'Britishness', as much as 'curriculum', is an imaginary" (Lawton 1975; Anderson 1991). Also 'nation-ness' is described as a "'cultural artefact of a particular kind' (p. 4), for which we need to examine carefully its history in order to understand its power." (Mills, 2018)

When deconstructing the curriculum, the research defined it as "'essentially a selection from the culture of a society'..., begging the question of who makes the cultural selection of knowledge and why....Much scholarship shows that curriculum practices often represent the values of dominant groups and played a key role within colonial curricula (Apple 1990; Kanu 2006a) ..." (Mills, 2018)

Further, in showing the power of the school curriculum, the report states "Since the British school curriculum is part of the narrative of the nation's culture, historical analysis is required to understand the sources and purposes of its cultural values, and to ask whose interests they serve (Tomlinson 2015a)." (Mills, 2018)

When looking at the history of expanding the curriculum from private to state schools, it states the ..."acceptance of school knowledge as 'truth' and the simplification of complex concepts to make them accessible, the school curriculum for working class students took up the public school values of British patriotism, militarism, support for monarchy, imperialist expansion, racial superiority and Christian paternalism (Tomlinson 1989)." (Mills, 2018)

The report then explores the tussle to embed the [Imperial] curriculum, which has been renamed over the years, including: having mainly white teachers who were "exposed to the ethnocentric curriculum during their own school days" and who lacked training of / experience to teach "a multi-cultural, anti-racist curriculum...(Tomlinson 2008, 38)"; the "arrival in Britain...of people from former colonies [post-war]...presenting the need for curriculum change to prepare all students for life in a multi-cultural society (DES 1977; Swann 1985; MacPherson 1999; Parekh 2000; Ajegbo and DfES 2007; Goldsmith 2008;" ... the "strong opposition from nationalists determined to defend the white social order by 'preserv – [ing] an imperial notion of a British national identity from 'alien cultures' ' (Tomlinson 2008, 71–2)" (Mills, 2018)

The change to New Labour failed to challenge [conservative

policies] "and reform the culturally biased, ethnocentric and racist curriculum (Tomlinson 2008, 146), with the framing of immigration as a 'problem'. This stance perpetuated the emphasis on nationalism and patriotism conveyed by the Right in the past, with similar effect – marginalising ethnic minority communities whilst ignoring structural inequalities and material disadvantage." (Mills, 2018)

They incorporated research that names "school as a key institution in the colonisation of minds, and of inculcating inferiority in colonised and racialised young people… where race becomes a central mode of colonial and postcolonial governance (Tyler 2013, 42)." (Mills, 2018)

Historical Association members (a membership organisation founded in 1906 and based in London) argued that the draft History National curriculum "conveyed 'Anglo-centric bias' (2013 section 3), neglecting British, European and global history. Countries other than Britain were only referred to when subjected to Britain's 'triumphal' military impact. Racist language… ignored alternative value perspectives and Black British history (including immigration)." (Mills, 2018)

After the inner-city riots in Northern England in 2001 a Government report, The Cantle Report blamed that the "absence of interaction between mainly Muslim and non-Muslim communities led to lack of common identities and shared values." Later in 2005, in response to the 2005 London bombings "the Government identified…what we now understand as the 'Fundamental British Values'"… [where the] "dominant narrative… was…[the] 'Muslim problematic', whereby Muslims were understood as the other, both physically and ontologically…" (Mills, 2018)

In the report, British Values has been critiqued as to "why equality, anti-racism and social justice" are not included? "'British Values' confer a binary of insider/outsider as British/non-British (Elton- Chalcraft, et al. 2017, 41), thereby constructing a polarisation between 'good' and inferior 'other'. The 'British' pre-fix harks back to nostalgic sentiments of Empire, deflecting attention from the violent realities of race and religious inequality in British society, and,...working to psychically defend white privilege." (Mills, 2018)

"In his Critical Psychology of the Postcolonial, Derek Hook (a white South African scholar) (2012), writes that disavowal (as a clashing of ideas, wishes and anxieties) can illuminate the workings of the 'ideological functioning of racism', specifically addressing the co-existence (politically and individually) of often contradictory positions, for example, a professed view of tolerance alongside racist behaviour (p. 180)." (Mills, 2018)

To "mark the 799th anniversary of Magna Carta, then Prime Minister David Cameron, wrote an article on British values for the newspaper the Mail on Sunday. For Cameron, the principles of the Magna Carta 'shine as brightly as ever' because they paved the way for the values that 'make Britain, Britain', and therefore 'every child' should learn about it." They "are at the 'core of what it is to live in Britain' (Cameron 2014)." (Mills, 2018)

"Yet amongst the many things missing from his history of Britain, in which he sees rule of law as playing a key part, is awareness of how 'the violence of imperialism was legitimated in its being exercised through law' (Fitzpatrick 2011, 19). McBride (2016) traces how 'historical practices of British colonial rule' illustrate how 'rule of law was an element in the development of an unequal system of international economics, politics, and law.'" (Mills, 2018)

"In their retellings of Britain's history and exoneration of rule of law, David Cameron, Michael Gove, and Theresa May's... speeches and articles, as constellations of a British Values policy-ensemble, appear to exhibit a 'profound historical forgetfulness' and 'historical amnesia', that is for Stuart Hall (1978, 26) 'a decisive mental repression' which attempts to 'wipe out and efface every trace of the colonial and imperial past'. This is a 'forgetting to remember' (Bhabha 1994, 160) the 'exclusionary acts of symbolic and material violence that are central to many nation-making projects' (McDonald 2006, 308). Hesse (1997, 87) draws upon Derrida (1982, 213) to explore how this amnesia is part of a 'white mythology' that: has erased within itself the fabulous scene that has produced it, the scene that nevertheless remains active and stirring, inscribed in white ink, an invisible design covered over in the palimpsest." (Mills, 2018)

The research was helpful in understanding the bigger picture, as on top of our self-concept, our concept of others, our muted shared history, the hierarchy of race, we have the school curriculum. The vast majority of us rely on school as a basis for education and learning. Parents rely on the school system to support their children's growth. The "British school curriculum is part of the narrative of the nation's culture" and seen by many as 'truth'.

However, analysis of the curriculum by the White Rose Consortium deemed the curriculum "culturally biased, ethnocentric and racist." It teaches "British patriotism, militarism, support for monarchy, imperialist expansion, racial superiority and Christian paternalism (Tomlinson 1989)." Whilst many of those qualities might be culturally embraced, celebrated by some and embedded in the narrative, amongst them are imperialist expansion and racial superiority.

In thinking about 'imperialism', – which is "a policy or ideology of extending the rule or authority of a country over other countries and peoples, often by military force or by gaining political and economic control." (Dictionary.com, 2019) I wonder how do you psychically hold this without the notion of superiority / inferiority?

The 'British Values' curriculum "doesn't teach about equality, anti-racism and social justice", but confers a "binary of insider/ outsider as British/non-British." (Elton- Chalcraft, et al. 2017, 41)."

So, we have this ever-perpetuating cycle, the curriculum being part of the culture and being seen as 'truth'.

Ahead of reading this research, I was going to revisit the chapter on 'A difficult Past' and expand on how I believe in filtering and suppressing this past, the operation of defence mechanisms have come in to play. However, after reading the above research, I feel this is more fitting for this chapter.

Defence mechanisms are ways that we operate unconsciously to deflect, avoid, or decrease uncomfortable, 'unacceptable', or difficult emotions. There are many types of defence mechanisms we can use to aid in avoiding uncomfortable stimuli.

For most people, there is an awareness of our shared history and also the unspoken/ muted aspects of our colonial past. However, in attempts to distance ourselves from the difficult elements of history, in attempts to only remember the accomplishments and not fully the means to accomplish, we deny a whole element of history.

In denying things, they do not simply disappear, the things that we deny, merely operate in different ways. In counselling training, there was a book that was repeatedly recommended, called the 'Body Keeps the Score: : Mind, Brain and Body in the Transformation of Trauma' by Bessel van der Kolk (which I mentioned at the beginning of this book). The author explores that when there is a disconnect from traumatic events experienced by a person, their bodies 'keep the score' and this is remembered in various ways, including vivid traumatic memories, and sometimes disease. The book promotes healing from trauma, which can be accomplished by various therapies, including EDMR and 'integrating' the trauma, and in doing so, then beginning to have agency over it.

The prologue in his book starts "One does not have to be a combat soldier, or visit a refugee camp in Syria or the Congo to encounter trauma. Trauma happens to us, our friends, our families, and our neighbors. Research by the Centers for Disease Control and Prevention has shown that one in five Americans was sexually molested as a child; one in four was beaten by a parent to the point of a mark being left on their body; and one in three couples engages in physical violence. A quarter of us grew up with alcoholic relatives, and one out of eight witnessed their mother being beaten or hit." (Kolk, 2014)

I feel in disavowal of acknowledging the full scope of British history, the emotion of it has been projected out on to 'the other'. In the actual history, with the ability to carry out the acts of slavery and create the hierarchy of race, there would have been detachment and disavowal. However, when we avoid, evade or suppress experiences, we give impetus for the operation of defence mechanisms.

Defence mechanisms such as 'Denial', – where we 'negate sensory data to avoid awareness of the painful aspect of reality. We abolish the external reality'. I believe we can see denial, where in evading looking at the difficult parts of the past, "Disavowal and distantiation have been crucial mechanisms facilitating avoidance and evasion." (Hall, 2013)

There is the defence mechanism of 'Distortion', – 'a reshaping of the external reality to suit inner needs and sustaining feelings of superiority and entitlement.' I believe we can see this in the history told, which has become embedded in the psyche of the nation, – where school is "a key institution in the colonisation of minds, and of inculcating inferiority in colonised and racialised young people."

There is also the defence mechanism of 'Projection', where 'the intolerable and unacceptable feelings about one's self cannot be held or owned'. These feelings are therefore projected out onto the other. It is more manageable to face what is deemed as contemptible, if it is placed out there, away from self. In doing so one can process through being appalled, one can grapple with the discomfort, from 'a safe place'. We can see this in creating 'the other', who is to be blamed, such as the 'Muslim problematic' (Mills, 2018) or the immigrant.

Being 'controlling' is a defence mechanism, of 'managing or regulating the environment excessively to avoid anxiety'. We can observe this through the managing and regulating through media messaging, through policy, to keep at bay the anxiety that might be felt about the other.

Rationalization, – 'offering rational explanations to justify attitudes, beliefs, behaviours instinctually based.' I believe we can see this in not acknowledging the bias that is felt, but creating policies to rationalize the bias felt, i.e. stop and search for black males; embedding 'British Values' into the school curriculum to counter-terrorism; holding South Asians responsible for the escalation of Coronavirus, in the North of England, withouth factoring in systemic inequalities.

So, through the lens of this filtered history, which becomes embedded in the minds of the nation through the curriculum, we have this implicit learnt narrative, which continues to be expressed in press reporting. It is a narrative which so focuses on 'the other', in looking at the race of 'the other', the religion of 'the other', the actions of 'the other', whilst endorsing white as 'the norm', therefore conferring a "binary of insider/outsider as British/non-British (Elton- Chalcraft, et al. 2017, 41)."

For example, to indicate the depth, embedded and implicit nature of this practice, consider the reaction when John Snow attached colour to the 'Leave Means Leave' rally, in calling demonstrators 'white'. There was great offence and huge outrage in John Snow linking actions to the white race. Complaints were made to Ofcom, and Channel 4 apologised for his comment.

"For those of us from the white majority, anti-racism needs to be more than just about 'valuing diversity' and marching or campaigning against racism. It also needs to be about us working to unravel our own white privilege...The concept of white privilege also implies the right to assume the universality of one's own experiences, whilst marking others out as different or abnormal. Seeing non-white people as 'ethnic' or 'exotic' while perceiving oneself as 'normal'. This ability of white people to call everybody else 'the other' and insist that whiteness is the default, the 'normal' is even more of a problem in the UK than it is in the US." (Gregg, 2014)

We have a narrative which, in refusal to look at the past, projects the intolerable onto the other, in demonising the other. The words of Brené Brown come to mind, "Here's what we know from the research," says Brown, "blame is simply the discharging of discomfort and pain. It has an inverse relationship with accountability. Blaming is a way that we discharge anger... Blame is faster than accountability: Accountability is a vulnerable process that takes courage and time." (Brown, 2011)

In keeping with the taught "culturally biased, ethnocentric and racist curriculum (Tomlinson 2008, 146), immigration is framed as a 'problem'. The 'illegal' migrant, ...pushes refugee seekers out from the humanitarian and rights-based realm and pulls them into [a] racialised and criminalised sphere. It switches their status from at-risk individuals deserving of safety and security to those who are risks, criminals and a source of insecurity, -one that needs to be detected, controlled and stopped from entering or living in the country." (Monish Bhatia, 2018)

"Migrants - when at all quoted - tend to be assigned lower credibility and less prominence than majority group speakers, whose credibility is usually enhanced and taken for granted. In (introductions to) quotations, verbs and adverbs are chosen which reinforce negative stereotypes through the representation of the out-group as a threat and as not respecting 'our' norms for civilised debate (Ter Wal, 1996)...Nominalisations, use of intransitive verbs, of passive voice and omission of the agent are used in order to conceal in-group agency in the portrayal of negative acts, e.g. of the police, or discrimination. On the other hand, agency and ethnic identity are used in headlines in which 'they' are associated with negative topics (illegal entry, protests, and crime). Minorities are thus presented in a role of active, responsible agents, and not victims (Graber, 1980, Fowler et al, 1979, van Dijk, 1991)." ((ERCOMER), 2002)

There is such a driven narrative and disdain for 'illegal' migrants/ immigrants that it fueled debates and the vote on Brexit / leaving the EU.

I remember going on holiday recently to Portugal and meeting some Brits abroad. It was a remote hotel, so the guests would sit in the bar in the evening. On this occasion, there were 6 of us that were sitting in the bar and chatting throughout the evening.

We made the mistake of venturing into talking about politics! Immigration came up, and the force with which things in the UK were blamed on immigration was incredible. One woman complained that her nearest hospital was 50 miles from her home and blamed this on immigration. I challenged her as to why immigration was responsible for this. Another of the men was so passionately talking about the boats that were attempting to cross the sea. He passionately said, and I will never forget the depth, anger and almost 'hatred' in which he said it, that if there is another boat of immigrants found they should be thrown into the sea!! On speaking with this man, I challenged him and challenged his perspectives on how he feels his life was personally impacted by immigration? I said everyone buys these arguments without challenge and there are no winners in this. You are left angry, and the immigrants are hated.

"Discourse analysis has shown how news definitions build on the dominant perspective of the powerful and on a mutual reinforcement of official and popular perspectives on the definition of social problems. This approach assumes that discourse plays a crucial role in the reproduction of ethnic prejudice and racism, because beliefs and opinions about ethnic out-groups become socially shared through communication and language use. Because most in-group members do not have a daily inter-action with immigrants, their beliefs and knowledge about the out-group are shaped largely by the media (van Dijk, 1987, …).” ((ERCOMER), 2002)

There are many ways in which the other is portrayed, including the black person/ black male. Thankfully, things have shifted in the UK in terms of imaging since the death of George Floyd. There seems to be a flurry of including us in advertising, which is positive. We are starting to hear more stories of an inclusive history. It was moving to see on This Morning, on daytime TV in the UK, a screen which said Black Lives Matter, which they used for a minute’s silence after the killing of George Floyd. There have been lots of other shifts to be more open and inclusive.

I know until now, there has been a long painful battle of being seen as ‘the other’ and all the themes that accompany this, in-cluding being dehumanised. How does this play out, there is the element of using colour to link to crime, to create negative as-sociations with being black. “Using ‘black’ and ‘white’ as racial identifiers can contribute to a micro-aggression because it spe-cifies individuals to a specific group. If using the specifier sug-gests that a particular group has, gives or receives superior or demeaning messages in contract to other group identification, it could be considered as a racial micro-aggression.” (Kulasze-wicz, 2015)

There are negative representations of black males, which has enormous consequences. Distortions “in the media are ul-timately significant because of the real-world effects they have on black males’ outcomes, which can be negatively affected any time a black male is in a position where his fate depends on how he is perceived by others, particularly whites, or on what kind of rapport he has with them. The real-world effects al-luded to… include everything from less attention from doctors to harsher sentencing by judges, lower likelihood of being hired for a job or admitted to school, lower odds of getting loans, and a higher likelihood of being [killed] by police." (Topos Partnership, 2011)

As we know, negative representations of black people in the press, at the macro-level, continue to influence outcomes and interactions at the micro-level. Seeing the horrific dynamic of George Floyd, being killed in front of our eyes was terrible and hearing him call out that he could not breathe. This incident was captured on film and sparked outrage in people observing the inhumane way in which he was treated. Unfortunately, in the UK, there has been an issue of black people dying in police custody and their families then trying to fight, often unsuccessfully, for justice. "The media shares no small part in denying justice for the bereaved. Invariably, where one would expect the media to investigate police wrongdoing in a suspicious death in custody, the dead themselves are smeared as too strong, too volatile or too alien for their own good, and so having brought their death upon themselves. The police are able to frame the death in terms of a media narrative that portrays race, and not racism, as the problem. As family and community campaigns for justice emerge, police and the media collude to define their demands as extremist and therefore illegitimate. A potential crisis of legitimacy for the police is deflected by the press." (Erfani-Ghettani, 2018)

Media has huge influence. Many people rely on it as a source of information, connecting us to social and political events, we may otherwise be unable to access. "Media educates people, with and without credible knowledge. School of Social Work Dean Larry Davis from the University of Pittsburgh was quoted saying that, 'One of the most important things any group of people can do is to control the image of themselves' (Barlow, 2011, paragraph 3)."..."Media holds significant influence in our daily lives, and it infiltrates our perceptions and understanding with continuous messages that impact our belief and value systems." (Kulaszewicz, 2015)

We, therefore, receive news through the cultural lens of the journalist. However, when this confers a binary insider/ outsider narrative, without consideration of the consequences at a micro and macro level for the 'outsider' it is problematic. For example, an article published in the Fordham Law Review looked at the "unconscious discrimination [which] helps explain the 'terrorists are Muslim' narrative..." (Corbin, 2017). This is used by employing two false narratives in news reporting. The "first is the idea that 'all terrorists are Muslim,' which sometimes even morphs into 'all Muslims are terrorists.' The second is that 'white people are never terrorists.' Neither are true. (Corbin, 2017) However, these narratives of insider/ outsider are streamed in reporting.

There are other insider / outsider narratives, such as expat v immigrant.

There is also the element of objectifying and sexualizing the black woman, which to me echo's stories of Sarah Baartman, the black South African woman, who was paraded naked in London, Ireland and Paris so people could stare at her body. Sarah lived in poverty, whilst the men who displayed her profited. Even in death, her remains were displayed in a museum, for people to stare at.

We have also the perpetuating of the stereotype of the angry black woman or aggressive black woman, which becomes embedded in the psyche of the nation and has a massive impact on interactions and having to work against this stereotype. Professor Uta Quasthoff (a discourse analyst) "defines the term stereotype as a verbal expression of a certain conviction or belief directed towards a social group or an individual as a member of that social group. The stereotype is typically an element of common knowledge shared to higher degree in a particular culture (see Quasthoff 1987: 786, 1978). It takes the logical form of a judgement that attributes or denies, in an oversimplified and generalising manner and with an emotionally slanted tendency, particularly qualities or behavioural patterns to a certain class of persons (Quasthoff 1973: 28)." (Reisigl, 1999)

In terms of the "real-world effects alluded to [which] include everything from less attention from doctors to harsher sentencing by judges (Topos Partnership, 2011)", I will expand a little further on this in the following chapter on 'How Implicit Bias Manifests in our Systems'. I will talk about how my 86-year-old aunt was 'perceived' as 'aggressive' whilst in hospital late last year, and talk about the treatment she received as a consequence!

HOW IMPLICIT
BIAS MANIFESTS
IN OUR SYSTEMS

Durable Inequality Theory

A s alluded to previously, there is much pain and trauma experienced as a black person, living within and navigating through the institutionally biased systems in the UK. This pain was captured in the focus groups and interviews, along with a hopefulness, when looking at and discussing the progress that has already been accomplished thus far. For example, many of our parents when arriving in the UK could not easily access financial services, and so created ingenious ways of saving, such as creating the pardoner system, where each person saving, would contribute a designated amount of money each month. Each member of the group would receive funds collected at the rota'd time.

There are also historical accounts of people such as Asquith Xavier, a black rail worker at Marylebone station. In as recent as 1966, Asquith Xavier applied for a job as a guard at Euston station but was declined as ethnic minority people were not allowed to work in jobs where they came into contact with the public. Asquith lobbied the union until eventually MPs and rail managers took notice, and he eventually got his victory. However, he then received death threats which he had to navigate through. There is now a plaque in Euston station to commemorate his achievement of successfully fighting to become the first black worker employed as a train guard.

We have, therefore come a long way, and this was acknowledged in the focus groups, as well as a sense of optimism for the future.

If ever there was research found which helped to understand the pain, distress and trauma, that I will describe in this chapter, which has led to nervous breakdowns and stress, amongst other things. If ever there was research which vindicates the experiences felt both personally and expressed in the groups and interviews, it was Charles Tilly's Durable Inequality Theory, found when researching for this book. In fact, if I did not write anymore on this chapter and pointed people to his theory, it would help in substantiating the expressions of BAME people that are so often silenced and refuted, when they try to challenge bias within organisations.

In terms of having expressions of experiencing racial bias rebuffed, I read a BBC article recently on 'Racial Gaslighting', and I thought it was interesting. Many of us are familiar with the term Gaslighting, which hinges on the film with the same title, in which a man tries to convince his wife she is going mad and tries to persuade her that real events are only in her imagination.

The article says that "Racial gaslighting often comes about when a victim is led to doubt and question their own sense of reality with regard to racism, says Seattle University's Angelique Davis, who's carried out a lot of research on the subject. Abusers will make them question their own judgement through victim blaming, policing their tone of voice, denial, dismissiveness and manipulation." (BBC, 2020)

Different techniques are used to gaslight someone racially. Some of those include: "countering someone's memory of events, withholding 'understanding' or refusing to listen, conveniently 'forgetting' or denying that something happened, playing down a person's feelings as unimportant or irrational, diverting to focus on credibility of what someone is saying and victim-blaming." (BBC, 2020)

This rebuffing, or 'Racial Gaslighting' is common. Indeed, when you attempt to challenge experiences and link events to your known experience of racism, you are often doubted, accused of playing the race card, having a chip on your shoulder, etc., etc.

In summarizing Charles Tilly's theory, pulling out themes relevant to this writing, Tilly looks at 'categorical inequalities' -- that is, inequalities across groups of people defined by relatively rigid social discriminators. "Durable inequality depends heavily on the institutionalization of categorical pairs...Relevant social categories include gender, race, immigrant status, or rural-urban origins." (Society, 2012)

"A category is a group of people sharing a boundary that distinguishes them from, and relates them to, a group of people excluded by such a boundary. These categories often have binary and unequal relationships: women/men, black/white, employer/employee, citizen/non-citizen, physician/nurse, Muslim/non-Muslim, etc." (Bhopal, n.d.)

Tilley's theory accounts for "how social categories often result in categorical inequalities. Not all categorical distinctions among people result in economic or political disparities across the resulting groups -- for example, 'good sense of humor/bad sense of humor' doesn't appear to result in income disparities across the humorous and the humorless. But the male-female wage gap, the black-white wealth gap...are examples of inequalities that follow from, and are presumably caused by, the categorical status possessed by the two groups." (Society, 2012)

Outside of the theory, when looking at disparities in socio-economic differences, it was stated: "discrimination has been an important conceptual vehicle for explaining ethnic inequalities in health and the role of socio-economic differences."... "If we want to tackle discrimination, we need to understand why it is occurring. Psychologists have explained the occurrence of discriminatory beliefs by intrapsychic factors such as racial animus or group closure. Recent European surveys show that racial or ethnic stereotyping is still rife..." (Bhopal, n.d.) The relational concept between the various categories is important to consider in understanding inequalities.

Organisations then either "create or sustain categorical inequality by means of the four basic mechanisms" (Bhopal, n.d.)

- Exploitation
- Opportunity hoarding
- Emulation
- Adaptation

"Exploitation occurs when an elite group" (Bhopal, n.d.) or "powerful, connected people command resources from which they draw significantly increased returns by coordinating the efforts of outsiders whom they exclude from the full value added by that effort." (Society, 2012)

Opportunity hoarding "operates when members of a categorically bounded network acquire access to a resource that is valuable, renewable, subject to monopoly, supportive of network activities, and enhanced by the network's modus operandi." (Society, 2012) For instance "the high concentration of Filipino nurses in Austria, Ecuadorian cleaning ladies in Madrid, Congolese priests in Belgium or South Asian optometrists in the UK." (Bhopal, n.d.)

Internal categorical inequalities (such as professor/ students or line manager/ staff) are then matched to external categorical inequalities (such as men/women or white/non-white), which keeps the whole structure durable.

Organizations whose survival depends on exploitation, therefore, tend to adopt categorical inequality.

"Because organizations adopting categorial inequality deliver greater returns to their dominant members and because a portion of those returns goes to organizational maintenance, such organizations tend to crowd out other types of organizations." (Society, 2012)

Emulation and adaptation are two further mechanisms that stabilize and perpetuate these inequalities. Emulation is the copying of established organisational models from one setting to another, for example, when women are more likely to work as the secretary of a white male manager in business settings, this may be emulated in the public sector.

Adaptation is a routine that facilitates social interaction, such as the tea break, peers lunching together, jokes and stories; these interactions ensure the normalisation of structural inequalities within day-to-day discourse. "The social group formed by adaptation acts to exclude other categories of people by, for example, making them feel uncomfortable, by conversations that are not pertinent, or disrespectful, to the excluded, e.g. chatting about drinking alcohol and partying, in the presence of Muslims who are forbidden to consume alcohol by their religion. (Bhopal, n.d.)

So, in terms of considering the theory above and looking at the practical ways that this plays out and is felt as a BAME person, navigating through institutions in the UK, I will revisit the focus groups which my cousin carried out many years ago. The focus groups were held for BAME women to understand their experiences, organizational change and steps to career progression. I shared earlier in this book that common themes that emerged were being left out and corporate decisions being made in social environments from which they had been excluded. I would say this is the Adaption stage of Charles Tilley's theory.

As mentioned, I recently held focus groups and interviews to explore 'How Implicit Bias Manifests in our Systems in the UK'. Participants were given the following definition of implicit Bias:

Defining Implicit Bias

Also known as implicit social cognition, implicit bias refers to the attitudes or stereotypes that affect our understanding, actions, and decisions in an unconscious manner. These biases, which encompass both favorable and unfavorable assessments, are activated involuntarily and without an individual's awareness or intentional control. Residing deep in the subconscious, these biases are different from known biases that individuals may choose to conceal for the purposes of social and/or political correctness. Rather, implicit biases are not accessible through introspection.

The implicit associations we harbor in our subconscious cause us to have feelings and attitudes about other people based on characteristics such as race, ethnicity, age, and appearance. These associations develop over the course of a lifetime beginning at a very early age through exposure to direct and indirect messages. In addition to early life experiences, the media and news programming are often-cited origins of implicit associations. (race, 2015)

Participants were sent the following questions for discussion:

1. Do you feel there is an implicit bias around race in the UK?

2. What causes you to answer yes – or no/ how do you substantiate your answer?

3. If you do/ do not feel there is an implicit bias around race in the UK –do you have any stories, either observed or personally experienced, to evidence whether or not there is implicit bias, that you are willing to share

4. What do you think is the impact of living in a society, where there is implicit bias around race (e.g. psychologically; emotionally; physically)?

5. If you do think there is an implicit bias around race in the UK/ what do you feel are the tools necessary to overcome, live within this?

6. If you do/ do not feel there is an implicit bias around race in the UK – how do you think this is evident/ manifests in our systems (e.g. prisons; housing; health; careers, etc.)?

7. How do you feel implicit bias manifests in our interactions, both intercultural (between different cultures) and intracultural (between same/ similar cultures)?

8. What do you think are the impacts of implicit bias on communities?

9. What do you feel are steps we can make to overcome/challenge implicit bias?

Firstly, in response to the 1st question 'Do you feel there is an implicit bias around race in the UK' there was a resounding explicit yes to the experience of implicit bias. Whether there was the existence of implicit bias was not even debatable in the interviews. It was deemed Implicit Bias was "part of the lived experience in the UK" and "not really a conversation to be had", "the question was more about why it had persisted and what ways are there to tackle it".

In addition to the experience shared earlier in the book, of observing other senior professionals in public service roles have breakdowns, ensuing from the treatment they experienced and unfair disciplines, there were other themes that emerged. There was a consistent and resounding theme of struggling to be promoted and working against ceilings. I have to say in all of my working life, this is a theme that I know experientially and have seen mapped out. I once supported an organisation that assisted companies in implementing diversity and saw the organisation chart of a well-known company, with all of the BAME employees in a bottleneck at the bottom of the organization. These people were educated, capable and frustrated.

Whilst there are those that make it to CEO and senior roles, there are consistent themes of blocks around progression. Participants expressed the "unconscious, implicit biases that exist"; "awareness of how black people, people of colour were struggling to be promoted"; how BAME peoples "skills and abilities were not being recognised". People talked about the impact on self on knowing you are capable, but having "blocks on moving forward" and how they were left feeling "hurt", "angry", "not good enough", and "incapable".

Participants talked about the impact on their mental health, being left questioning whether they were good enough, and "the major emotional impact" of being "suppressed in work". Participants felt they were giving their all, with little reward. The causes for not being promoted could not be substantiated by employers, and it was observed white colleagues who had the same attributes as the reasons given to participants for non-promotion, were promoted.

An article published in the British Journal of Psychiatry says: "Racism is a form of discrimination that stems from the belief that groups should be treated differently according to phenotypic difference. It is widespread in the UK (Modood *et al*, 1997). Racism has many forms; direct attack is less common than perceived discrimination in interpersonal communication, or inequity in the receipt of services or justice." (McKenzie, 2002)

The article continues: "Researchers mainly conceptualised racism is a stressor. An individual's perception of society as racist and the experience of everyday minor attack minor acts of discrimination are thought to constitute a chronic stressor. Individual, more overtly racist acts are considered as life events (acute stressors) that are superimposed on this chronic stress (Bhugra & Cochrane, 2001)." (McKenzie, 2002)

"Institutional racism is often indirect. An institution may not set out to discriminate but through its rules, may have this very effect...In the UK, widespread discriminatory social policy may influence the rates of mental illnesses, their presentation and outcome..." "Mental health research into the effects of racial discrimination runs the risk of medicalising appropriate social struggle and distress...It has been argued that there should be a closer examination of those bodies that discriminate, rather than their victims." (McKenzie, 2002)

Attendees talked about feeling the existing system was "toxic", "racist", "prejudiced" and "stressful". That in addition to the impact of living with this toxic, unequal dynamic, there are the other things that we have to manage in being human, so "we have a double whammy of exposure".

I guess these participants were expressing how it feels to be the recipients of the 'exploitation' mechanism of Charles Tilley's Durable Inequality Theory. In this phase of the process, the "elite group" (Bhopal, n.d.) or "powerful, connected people command resources from which they draw significantly increased returns by coordinating the efforts of outsiders whom they exclude from the full value added by that effort." (Society, 2012)

Participants in the focus groups expressed the impact on self-esteem, confidence, self-doubt, emotional impact, health and the psychological impact that occurred from "giving your all" and working in a system where you are hindered from progression.

Another theme that emerged from the focus groups is the implicit belief that black people are not "seen" as leaders. I think this, as well as the Exploitation, Opportunity Hoarding, Emulation and Adaptation phases, are demonstrated in the Boardrooms of FTSE 100 companies.

Other themes that emerged from female participants were navigating against the stereotype of being the "aggressive black woman", as mentioned previously and having to navigate relationships with white male and female colleagues due to being accused of being "aggressive".

To demonstrate how deeply embedded this stereotype is, and how you really don't need to do much to be put into that box, I will tell you the story of my 86-year-old aunt, who was labelled as "aggressive"!

My 86-year-old aunt was in London over the Christmas period in 2019, staying with family. She lives in Luton and has lived there since she came to Britain in the 60s.

Whilst in London, she unfortunately had a seizure, caused by diabetes, the 1st one she has ever experienced. She was taken to hospital by ambulance, with flashing blue lights. I was in the ambulance with her. The ambulance crew were incredible and amazingly calm. They were treating her seizure with such composure, whilst I feared the worse.

She ended up being in ICU for a while and then coming out. My aunt is an 86-year-old lady, very thin, about a size 6 – 8 at the time, as she had lost weight in hospital. She was making a good recovery and a couple of days later, had woken up by herself and was looking very bright. She was then moved out of ICU.

However, when I arrived at the hospital the following day, her son and the rest of the family were there, I could not believe the sight in front of me. Her son, my cousin saw my expression, the shock was written all over my face! and said 'yes'! My aunt had been heavily sedated!!

She was sedated to the point where her mouth was open, head turned to one side, and she looked like she had massively deteriorated from the day before. We were told that my aunt was being 'aggressive'.

I understand that my aunt was in hospital. I get the picture of an overstretched, busy hospital ward, with little staff. Apparently, she had been talking and quite understandably wanted to walk around. The ward was too busy, and the staff did not have capacity to deal with this, so what did they do, they heavily sedated her. As mentioned, they deemed that she was 'aggressive'.

We then entered an ongoing battle of trying to bring her back to health. We explained to the hospital staff that we did not want her to be sedated. We asked that if she was 'aggressive' to call one of us, and we would come to the hospital to support, assist and calm her. They asked did we want to get a call in the middle of the night? We responded, yes.

My cousin, her son, then decided he would sit in the hospital daily, to be at his mum's bedside, to liaise with staff and stop the cycle of sedation. He expressed his wishes clearly to staff for his mum not to be sedated.

This worked temporarily. Another cousin joined him at the hospital. The other cousin, there to support in requesting my aunt not be sedated, arrived at the hospital dressed smartly with a suit jacket. He did so, as he expressed, he knew how black males could be perceived. He wanted to negotiate to try to connect and get the best care for my aunt.

There was a slight reprieve, due to negotiations, where my aunt was not sedated. However, the following day, after sitting by my aunt's bedside, both cousins decided to go to the family room, to get something to eat. When they arrived back from getting a sandwich, she had again been heavily sedated.

Suddenly in entering this particular hospital system, she was labelled as aggressive, and the approach was to sedate her. If this is what happens to an 86-year-old frail black woman, what hope is there for anyone that is younger, or stronger?

The issue is: we have institutions which are set up in society. These institutions are operated by people. We have a media narrative which continues to endorse social representations inspired by the school curriculum, which confers "a binary of insider/outsider as British/non-British (Elton- Chalcraft, et al. 2017, 41), thereby constructing a polarisation between 'good' and inferior 'other'". (Mills, 2018) We are encouraged to have negative associations to race and religion, e.g., black, and Muslim as well as embedding stereotypes.

Obviously, not everyone will operate like this, but people are the faces of the institutions, the one on one contacts, which either open doors or close doors. These are the faces and points of interaction, in the hospitals, the mental health institutions, the shops, the employers, the banks, the call centres on the phone, etc.

Other themes that emerged from the focus groups and interviews were having to use an English sounding middle name when applying for jobs, rather than an 'African' name. There was a reference to studies that have been done in having identical CVs and qualifications but changing the name, and the inference that CVs are rejected because of an ethnic-sounding name.

Other themes that emerged were going into the school system as an external person and being continually reminded of the 'insidious institutional racism'. Also, (as Akala the academic and rapper has identified), the benefit of having Saturday schools for BAME children to bring some balance to the curriculum taught in schools.

There was also the question of talking to our children to prepare them for 'mainstream society, racial socialisations and the corporate world', in a similar way that African Americans speak to their children about how to interact with the police.

George Floyd

I was totally overwhelmed at watching the killing of George Floyd, as many people were. It is disturbing that a person could be treated and die in this way, let alone the unimaginable trauma and pain there must be for his family.

In reaction to his death, whilst I do not condone looting, (although local reports were adamant agent provocateurs were carrying this out), people protesting on the streets obviously felt impacted by his killing. However, we then had Donald Trump, president of the US tweeting "when the looting starts, the shooting starts." Aside from the historical associations of these words, it obviously authorises and incentivises further killings of citizens.

This is the reality of life on the ground within a biased system. The very structures that are designed to protect and assist citizens, work against you. The police said George Floyd was resisting arrest, whilst a separate video shows him operating and walking with police, without resisting. The police officer whilst murdering him then says, so casually without care or emotion to 'get up then'. These are the experiences we go through of systemic injustice, being told one thing, when you clearly know that is not the truth or the case. How can he get up when a policeman is sitting on his throat?

You can see passers-by pleading for the police to let him get up. The natural response of wanting to help someone would be to go in and physically assist. However, you can see the resistance of the passers-by, especially one black man. There seems to be the intrinsic knowledge that if you step in and try to help, the brutal force of this system could come down upon you. You could be the person that ends up on the floor, with the police officers, 'upholders of the law', kneeling on your neck.

Whilst all of this is happening, life goes on, people watch, they are powerless to help. The only help is the power of social media, as videos circulate, which then caused outrage. If the event were not documented on film, there would have been no consequence for the officers that killed him. Even with events having been documented and sparking global outrage, there seems to be resistance in the officers being held accountable.

These are the experiences we face in institutions every day, which are meant to be there to support, protect and develop us, such as schools, hospitals, the police forces, workplaces, etc. etc. These are the familiar experiences, where there are barriers, blocks, excuses and indiscretions, the 'systemic' word against yours. We are underrepresented in the places we long to be in. We are overrepresented in the places that we do not want to be in.

I was so overwhelmed by the video; I didn't know how to process what I had watched. How could a person be murdered like that on the street? How could a police officer, who is in a position of 'upholding the law', treat a person in that way, with such blatant disregard and coldness! How could you have a person underneath you and be so cut off and cold about that person? It was really disturbing to see.

There has been a long historical debate to add 'racism' to the DSM5 scale. The DSM5 scale (Diagnostic and Statistical Manual of Mental Disorders, 5th Edition) "was created to enable mental health professionals to communicate using a common diagnostic language." (NHS, 2013) There has been criticism about the DSM 5 due to "an increasing tendency to "medicalise" patterns of behaviour and mood that are not considered to be particularly extreme" (NHS, 2013)

In addition to absolving personal responsibility, opinions against adding racism to the DSM 5 scale argue that like "violence, considering racism as a symptom highlights the reality that such behavior is multidetermined and complex. However, unlike violence, DSM-IV-TR (APA, 2000) does not specifically include racism as a potential symptom of various disorders. This inattention and denial of racism in The Diagnostic and Statistical Manual of Mental Disorders has made it impossible to track this extremely destructive set of mental phenomena. With the DSM-5 moving toward the use of dimensional disorders instead of categorical disorders, it would be difficult to delineate racism or xenophobia as a specific categorical disorder. However, it would be possible to place the symptom on a trait scale. This would require scientific rigor to determine the validity and reliability of racism as a symptom or a personality trait." (Bell, 2013)

"Owing to the pervasiveness of racism in society, it is evident that racist feelings, thoughts, and behaviors are, in part, a product of socially transmitted learned behavior (Bell, 2004). Those viewing racism as a social ill, in which racist patterns are institutionalized, taught, and internalized through socialization, believe that the proper approach to this social ill lies in politics and social change, and not in the diagnostic and interpretive techniques of psychiatry (Fannon, 1967; Thomas & Sillen, 1972). Racism in this regard is placed within a systems and biological perspective. It, thus, can be thought of as the systematic overvaluing of assumed inherent differences. These differences are based on physiognomic characteristics driven by genetics. This way of thinking establishes the basis of a declared or hidden dominance-submission system in which the oppressor explicitly or tacitly shapes and controls the perceptions of the victim (Carter, 1994; Pierce, 1988, 1992; Shanklin, 1998)." (Bell, 2013)

Whilst I might reference and be informed by the DSM5 scale, as a counsellor I would never 'diagnose' or 'label' someone by the scale as this would be beyond my limits of proficiency. However, watching the video of the cold killing of George Floyd did make me recall and consider the argument.

As mentioned at the beginning of the book, your comments on Meghan Markle, were the reason I was prompted to write this book. The killing of George Floyd was the impetus to finish the book.

Like many people all over the world, I was so disturbed by watching the video. At the time, I did not know what to do with the overwhelm I felt and found writing about it cathartic. After seeing him killed, in cathartic expression and as a way to deal with the emotions of seeing him killed, I wrote words to him, to express how sorry I was for what I had seen. I was going to delete the words for the final edit of the book, but in rethinking felt I should leave them in here, as he was the reason, I wanted to finish this book.

In trying to process what I was feeling, I spent some time to take a few moments, to say some words, as if I were speaking to George Floyd. For me, it was the disturb of seeing a man so distressed; it seemed like he knew he was going to die. The distress of seeing him crying out for his mum. A grown man, so hurt, that he goes to a primal place and begins to call for his mum!

To see the fluids on the floor! I am not a physician, but to me, it seemed his body was shutting down and releasing fluids, a process the body goes through when dying. It almost felt like he was so distressed, his body was so distressed, it was as if his body was saying 'we are trying our best to cope with the lack of oxygen, everything is hurting, we are fighting to survive! We have no energy even to hold anything in our bowels, let go of this stuff.'

My words to him: "I'm so sorry son. I am so sorry young man that you had to experience this. I am so sorry that you had to experience this and to die in this way. I am sorry that you had to die in such a brutal way, in broad daylight, in the streets where you were meant to be free. In the land that you lived in and were meant to be free. I am sorry no one protected you. I am so sorry young man, son, that the men, the people who were meant to be proud citizens and upholders of the law; the men who were sworn into their roles in pride, to protect and serve their country, – did not protect you. I am so sorry that the men who treated you this way, did not see you as a man! That is their illness. But their illness hurt you. I am so sorry their illness and warped view, hurt you. The illness that saw you as less than. The illness that they did not see you as a man. The illness that they did not treat you with any worth. You have worth, and you are worthy. You are worthy of regard and honour. I am so sorry that you experienced this distress and pain, on the streets of America, -the land of opportunity, the land of the 'free'. I am sorry for your pain. I am hurt, that you hurt in this way. I am hurt, that you were hurt in this way!

I watched what happened to you on my screens. I only wish that this were not real and some distressing scene in a movie that I happened to see. My distress is, that this was not a movie; this was real life.

If it were a movie, I would have turned away or changed the channel. This is real life, and I am so moved by what I have seen, I have to write, to send thoughts to you, to even process what I have seen. My writing is a process to send out words to let you know how sorry I am this happened. It's also I guess a cathartic process to try to deal with what I have just seen.

I have just seen the news, so at the time of writing, I do not know anything about you. You may have been a father, a husband, a brother. You were clearly and obviously someone's son. You may have been a business owner, entrepreneur, I do not know. However details emerge about you, whether you are made out to be a criminal, even if you were, for me that is not relevant. What is relevant for me is that no-one should be treated with this much lack of regard. What an illness that is!

This is how I am aware men who look like you are treated George. We know it happens on the streets of America! Thank God you were filmed; otherwise, it would have been reported as another death in police custody. Death for black people in police custody is a familiar thing, even here in the UK, although my personal dealings with the police have been good. You find the person who 'died in custody' is often demonised. Thankfully, there was a video which showed you did not resist arrest!

We used to have a singer here in the UK, Smiley Culture, who was famous in the 80s, who died in police custody. Apparently, he stabbed himself in the heart!

This is how men like you are represented in many films; they are killed in the early scenes, disregarded, it's easier to kill the black man. Thankfully, the disregard is not always so extreme that it is a matter of life and death, but it's still there in many ways.

I am sorry and wanted to honour what I had seen in the book, regardless of the details that will emerge, as for me, they are irrelevant. I also think of your family too and want to send out prayers for their comfort, after such a distressing loss.

I am so sorry!

COVID-19

The Great Leveler or The Great Exposer

"**B**lack people are four times more likely to die than white people from COVID-19", came the sound of the news report. The tone of the reporter's voice sounded almost excited and relieved; it implied that she possibly felt now less at risk, during what has been a challenging time for many.

The tone of the reporting was not empathetic. It seemed to weaponize us and imply that we were physiologically disadvantaged and a strain in the battle against COVID.

In hearing the reports and discussing with friends and family, we wondered if that were the case, and the statistics were not limited to Britain and the US, why we were not dying in Africa and the Caribbean.

I was born in the UK and have lived my life here and I am very aware of the BAME experience of living in the UK. As per Durable Inequality Theory, and as per Robin DiAngelo's quote: "when a racial groups collective prejudice is backed by the power of legal authority and institutional control, it is transformed into racism, a far-reach system that functions independently from the intention or self-images of individual actors",

(DiAngelo, 2019).

In order to give some more background on this experience, as per keeping with this book, let's look at some of the research statistics, as per 2018, of the overall systemic experience of being BAME, and living in the UK, to bring some insight to the COVID-19 statistics.

Employment

- unemployment rates were significantly higher for ethnic minorities at 12.9 per cent compared with 6.3 per cent for White people
- Black workers with degrees earn 23.1 per cent less on average than White workers
- in Britain, significantly lower percentages of ethnic minorities (8.8 per cent) worked as managers, directors and senior officials, compared with White people (10.7 per cent) and this was particularly true for African or Caribbean or Black people (5.7 per cent) and those of mixed ethnicity (7.2 per cent)
- Black people who leave school with A-levels typically get paid 14.3 per cent less than their White peers

Education

- just 6 per cent of Black school leavers attended a Russell Group university, compared with 12 per cent of mixed and Asian school leavers and 11 per cent of White school leavers
- Black Caribbean and Mixed White/Black Caribbean children have rates of permanent exclusion about three times that of the pupil population as a whole

Crime

- rates of prosecution and sentencing for Black people were three times higher than for White people, 18 per thousand population compared with six per thousand population for White people
- for sentencing it was 13 per thousand population for Black people and five per thousand population for White people
- in England and Wales ethnic minority children and adults are more likely to be a victim of homicide
- the homicide rate for Black people was 30.5 per million population, 14.1 for Asian people and 8.9 for White people
- White women are more at risk of domestic abuse than ethnic minority women, with 7.4 per cent reported being victims of abuse compared with 4.4 per cent of ethnic minority women
- race hate crimes on Britain's railway networks have risen by 37 per cent
- in England, 37.4 per cent of Black people and 44.8 per cent of Asian people felt unsafe being at home or around their local area, compared with 29.2 per cent of White people

Living standards

- Pakistani or Bangladeshi and Black adults are more likely to live in substandard accommodation than White people
- 30.9 per cent of Pakistani or Bangladeshi people live in overcrowded accommodation, while for

Black people the figure is 26.8 per cent and for White people it is 8.3 per cent

- if you are an ethnic minority person, you are still more likely to live in poverty. Our evidence shows that 35.7 per cent of ethnic minorities were more likely to live in poverty compared with 17.2 per cent of White people

- in Scotland, ethnic minority households are more likely to experience overcrowding, with 11.8 per cent for ethnic minority households compared with 2.9 per cent for White households

Health and care

- Black African women had a mortality rate four times higher than White women in the UK

- there is a significant disproportionate number of ethnic minorities detained under mental health legislation in hospitals in England and Wales

- Black African women were seven times more likely to be detained than White British women

- Gypsies, Travellers and Roma were found to suffer poorer mental health than the rest of the population in Britain and they were also more likely to suffer from anxiety and depression

(EHRC, 2018)

Statistics from EHRC - https://www.equalityhumanrights.com/en/race-report-statistics

I am sure if you consider the statistics above, the news that black people are four times more likely to die from COVID-19, than white people, has some context! It is alarming to look at statistics of the macro systemic picture, but very much understood as an experience by many BAME people.

As per Durable Inequality Theory, institutional bias and racism, we often end up disproportionately working on front line roles. This obviously increases the risk of exposure to the virus, in addition to other factors.

The COVID-19 pandemic has been an extremely challenging time. On emerging, it was a new and unusual experience for all. It has been a difficult time for those whose income was affected, including the psychological impact and stress for many.

Families have had to school their children whilst working. Some people have really enjoyed the experience of being at home and reconnecting with family. For others, the home environment is an unsafe or stressful one.

This has been a virus which none of us has had experience with. We have seen an unusually high daily death toll previously, and all have had to adjust so that the NHS would not be overwhelmed with cases.

Some of us have lost loved ones and have been unable to bury or mourn them in the usual way. Weddings have been cancelled and businesses shut. The pandemic caused an atmosphere of fear, stress, anxiety, and loss whilst some have experienced reconnection, rest, and time with family.

We even had the queen give a speech in April, which she had also done during the war to encourage the nation. We truly have been living in unprecedented times.

At the same time, this all happened on the backdrop of Brexit and initially, there was scarcity with food and toilet paper in the shops. The nation was under pressure! It seems at times of pressure, Nationalism steps in. "On 6 April it was announced that the prime minister had been taken into St Thomas's hospital with Covid-19, and the next day he was moved into intensive care. By the time Johnson had re-emerged on 12 April with a video thanking the NHS staff who had saved his life, the mood had changed. Led by certain newspapers, the sense of measured proportionality that had governed public debate over the course of March was now lost, and an impassioned COVID nationalism was born." (Guardian, 2020)

The NHS became the national symbol that we all focused on. Each Thursday at 8 pm, people would lean out of windows, step outside and applaud the NHS. We were grateful for all the NHS workers were doing, fighting for lives, on the front line, during a frightening time where most people were advised to stay at home. Supermarkets and companies across the nation began to prioritise the NHS with access to products or services.

We had the strapline, "Stay home. Protect the NHS. Save lives." On exiting hospital, Boris Johnson said "We are making progress in this national battle because the British public formed a human shield around this country's greatest national asset – our National Health Service. We understood and we decided that if together we could keep our NHS safe, if we could stop our NHS from being overwhelmed, then we could not be beaten, and this country would rise together and overcome this challenge, as we have overcome so many challenges in the past." (Guardian, 2020)

We had entered a time of pulling together, solidarity, referencing the war, of Nationalism. However, with nationalism and British Values, 'the other' gets blamed.

"'British Values' confer[s] a binary of insider/outsider as British/non-British (Elton- Chalcraft, et al. 2017, 41), thereby constructing a polarisation between 'good' and inferior 'other'. The 'British' pre-fix harks back to nostalgic sentiments of Empire, deflecting attention from the violent realities of race and religious inequality in British society, and,...working to psychically defend white privilege." (Mills, 2018)

During this time, a friend of mine – a peer, who is a white English male – circulated a tweet by Steve Peers, the British academic and Professor in the School of Law at the University of Essex. In the tweet Steve referenced an article by the daily mail. The headline of the article was 'Let our teachers be hero's'. The article did not seem to be received well online, as people saw the daily mail as being divisive. The picture in the final article was of a smiling teacher sitting down with an open book, and a smiling child at her side. However, in the tweet, Steve Peers also showed the actual original image. In the original image, the teacher was with six children. The children around her were a diverse group, including BAME children. In the Daily Mail article, however, the other children were cropped out of the photograph. The remaining picture showed a white teacher, with a white child.

This in itself, could be seen as simple editing. However, as someone pointed out, one of the BAME children, who was standing closest to the child captured, in the original photograph, had been literally photoshopped out of the picture. As the person who noticed pointed out – the background remained, but the BAME child had been removed, – leaving an image of a white 'heroin' teacher, teaching a white child. As Steve Peers so eloquently titled his tweet 'Qwhite the photo cropping on that Daily Mail front page!'

As mentioned earlier in the chapter on 'A Difficult Past' BAME people were literally edited out and not captured in any of the images of our 'heroes' and our NHS staff. This is particularly hurtful when you consider the sacrifice that people have made over the years in supporting the NHS. It is upsetting when you think that the "NHS, like so much of postwar Britain, was built by immigrants and could not have survived in its current form without them. There were recruitment campaigns for nurses in Malaysia, Mauritius and elsewhere in the empire as well as the Caribbean. By 1971, 12% of British nurses were Irish nationals. By the turn of the century, 73% of the GPs in Wales's Rhondda valley and 71% in nearby Cynon valley were south Asian.

Today, roughly a third of the tier-2 visas for skilled migrants go to NHS employees." (Guardian, 2018)

As mentioned previously, I have never been into a hospital in London and seen an all-white staff base. Hospitals have a vast diversity of staff. Yet on news reporting, in representing the 'heroes' of the NHS, BAME people were erased from the picture.

It communicates a considerable amount that someone would take the time to photoshop out the image of a BAME child. It communicates much about the ethos, integrity and narrative of the reporting, to take the time to eliminate a person from a picture that does not fit the 'tone' of the message being presented of a hero.

In the UK, there are racial inequalities and disparities. These differences cause impacts on trauma, socioeconomic and health outcomes.

Professor Kimberley Thiedon, medical anthropologist, studies health disparities and situation biology's from structural inequalities and racism. In a COVID-19 talk on intersectionality, she talked about: "how life events and environmental exposures become embodied, in an individual's life span, and may cause intergenerational effects, via epigenetic changes among others." She says our "bodies are historical processes and historical sites, we see the sedimentation of centuries of inequality, right down to the cellular level." In the talk, she references the things that we are hearing a lot about during the pandemic, such as underlying conditions (diabetes, high blood pressure, asthma, stress-related illnesses). She says she wants to take that "a step further. What are the underlying structural conditions that shape disease occurrence, progression and outcome? Why is it that we see so many stress-related, tension-related illnesses in the African American population? Racism is a pathogen! We measure race, let's measure racism as the health risk. Discrimination and marginalization are public health risks, so the underlying conditions that produce situated biology's, and that unfairly distribute risk, are part of what we need to be thinking about." (Theidon, 2020)

In thinking about COVID-19 and us navigating through this unprecedented time, I was also thinking about the issue of facemasks. In considering the 'Triangle of Insight', 'back then', 'out there', 'in here', I wondered how the past 'back then', might be impacting the interactions 'out there' with the British public and facemasks?

I was considering that over the years, the media have quite literally vilified people who wear face coverings. There have been newspaper articles, radio phone in's, TV debates to discuss 'the other' who walk around with their faces covered.

All sorts of arguments have been used about the reasons people should not wear face coverings. Explanations have been that face coverings impacts on communication, respect, our values. Indeed, in one debate about the Hijab in 2017, it was argued "multiculturalism grants too much autonomy to group rights and communities are setting their own standards. The wearing of a facial cover or mask - for a mask is what it is - is now associated with groups within our society that wish to hide their identity from cameras and authority, and a reminder of the use of the balaclava by terrorists and criminals. Immigrants must be encouraged to adapt to the adopted cultural norms and this discussion should be widened to show the advantages of seeing clearly who we are trying to relate to." (Society, 2017)

However, now with coronavirus, after years of debates and reporting which demonise and vilify people who wear face coverings, we are being told we "must wear a face covering by law" (GOV.UK, 2020) in certain indoor settings. We are being encouraged to wear masks in other outdoor settings.

In terms of the psychodynamic model of the 'Triangle of Insight', I wonder how do you embed such hostility over the years into people's psyche around the attachment to what a face covering represents, and then suddenly want a majority complicit public to wear masks?

Further, in terms of the historical 'British Values' narrative which implies an 'ingroup/ outgroup, or binary insider/ outsider' (Mills, 2018), there is the dynamic of local lockdowns and spikes in cases, which to date have happened in Leicester and Blackburn.

It was reported a "Staggering 85% of new coronavirus infections in Blackburn 'are among South Asians...Dominic Harrison, the authority's director of public health, said 85 per cent of the 114 new cases were people from South Asian backgrounds. That's despite the South Asian community only accounting for 30 per cent of the council's 150,000 population. Many other areas of England which have the current highest infection rates of Covid-19, such as Bradford, Rochdale and Oldham, also have large South Asian communities." (Mail, 2020)

In the above reporting, we have the classic example of ingroup/ outgroup; the norm and 'the other' with blame apportioned to 'the other'.

Blackburn Councillor "Saima Afzal told the PA news agency: 'It should be a concern to anybody if any community is stigmatised'...He warned against analysing the statistics inaccurately as 'they can be twisted any way you want to portray them'. 'If you are going home and you are working and you are maybe not abiding by the rules as rigidly as you should be, and you go home and you are caring for a family member, or there are three or four families living under one household, because of economic reasons, or financial issues, and the Asian community do that - they pool their resources together to help the whole family survive.' 'If then they are going home, they are passing it on to more than one person... there's a cocktail of other factors as well...there's the inequalities that have been around for years.'" (Telegraph, 2020)

So, with the backdrop of COVID-19, there are many factors taking place. We seem to have reporting that is outcome-focused and doesn't address the input of systemic inequalities in Britain.

As per Charles Tilley's Durable Inequality Theory, with Exploitation and Opportunity Hoarding, BAME communities often end up working on front line roles. In finding ways to navigate systemic inequalities, as Blackburn Councillor Saima Afzal alluded to, 'Asian families pool together to help the whole family survive.' As a counsellor in reading that line, I think 'survive' is a poignant word to use, as you are quite literally surviving systemic "inequalities that have been around for years" (Telegraph, 2020)

I think a more honest conversation about COVID-19 reporting in relation to BAME communities, would be, as Professor Kimberley Thiedon says to take a look at what "are the underlying structural conditions that shape disease occurrence, progression and outcome?" (Theidon, 2020) Rather than blaming and weaponizing communities, a more honest look would be to consider the systemic treatment of BAME communities in the UK, the tip of which has been exposed during the pandemic.

MOVING FORWARD

Comparisons of Reporting on Meghan to the Racial Narrative

W hilst we all have to navigate through our personal lives and the challenges that brings, which are important and I am in no way undermining(!), as a BAME person in the UK, you are navigating through all the additional issues based around race.

For those who have never had to navigate around race, who have been "insulated from racial stress" (DiAngelo, 2019), it might be hard to grasp themes of systemic inequality, or that race might have played a part in the reporting of Meghan Markle.

I hope the themes explored in this book, have provided some insight into some of the issues attached to race, there are to navigate through.

In response to your comment, "Meghan and Harry haven't been criticiSed because of her colour but because she's a selfish social climber and he's a weak whiner - and by playing this despicable race card they have grossly libelled all of Britain" (Mail, 2020), I hope that the themes explored in this book, have illustrated some of the outworkings of implicit bias.

In terms of looking at the reporting on Meghan, in addition to the text in this book, I have tried to list some themes below, covered in this book, to substantiate why I believe the reporting on Meghan ties into themes of racial bias.

- She has been exoticized in reporting, a form of racial Microaggression. "Exoticization: (i.e., when people of color are objectified or treated as tokens). A common occurrence is when a man tells an Asian American woman that she is so 'exotic', or that 'he has an Asian fetish.'" (Nadal, 2014)

- In referring to Meghan as exotic, it immediately positions her as 'the other' and white as 'the norm'. This is a dynamic intrinsic to 'normalizing' whiteness and highlighting the other: "Seeing non-white people as 'ethnic' or 'exotic' while perceiving oneself as 'normal'" (Gregg, 2014). "Culture is often viewed as 'other' and black as unusual, exotic and 'cultural'. In this way, white/ whiteness is the dominant privileged norm and becomes both neutral and strangely invisible." (Naughton, 2006)

- As per Social Representations, from the school curriculum, embedded in the psyche of the nation, and which "is part of the narrative of the nation's culture" (Mills, 2018), and is accepted as 'truth', the reporting of Meghan confers "a binary of insider/ outsider as British/non-British (Elton- Chalcraft, et al. 2017, 41)..." (Mills, 2018) The reporting has had the connotation of insider (Royal Family and British) and outsider: Meghan

- She has been pathologized in reporting, another form of racial Microaggression. "Pathologizing Cultural Values: (i.e., when people of color are criticized for their communication styles, behaviors, styles of dress). For instance, when an Asian American or Latina/o is told to 'get rid of your accent', a subtle message is sent that one needs to assimilate...(New York: Wiley & Sons 2010)". (Nadal, 2014) For example, comments on the way she holds her bump, being demonised for eating avocados.

- The reporting of her mimics racist patterns which are "institutionalized, taught, and internalized through socialization...This way of thinking establishes the basis of a declared or hidden dominance-submission system in which the oppressor explicitly or tacitly shapes and controls the perceptions of the victim (Carter, 1994; Pierce, 1988, 1992; Shanklin, 1998)." (Bell, 2013) The reporting style certainly communicates an assumed dominance/submission dynamic.

- She has been dehumanized in the reporting! "Dehumanisation is the process by which conscious and unconscious bias leads people to see a racial minority as less human, – less worthy of respect, dignity, love, peace and protection. Psychology research finds that White police officers and young White students are more likely to see Black children as young as 10 years of age as being less worthy of protection and inviting violence in comparison to White children." (Zevallos, 2015)

- As per "the affective colonial architecture informing who could feel for whom in interwar Britain" (MATERA, 2016) and the hierarchy of race, which implicitly impacts interactions, there is no empathy for Meghan. Her white father's story, however, is treated with empathy and consideration. For example: "In one brief but explosive text message, Mr. Markle reveals his enormous pain, both physical and emotional..." (Morgan, 2020)

- As in keeping with research of discourse analysis and reporting on 'out groups', such as Migrants, the reporting on Meghan confers outgroup "threat and as not respecting 'our' norms..." (Ter Wal, 1996)

- As per the reporting of Minorities, Meghan is presented "in a role of active, responsible agent, and not [a] victim... (Graber, 1980, Fowler et al, 1979, van Dijk, 1991)" ((ERCOMER), 2002)

- As per the social construct of race, and the social representations of "British patriotism, militarism, support for monarchy, imperialist expansion, racial superiority and Christian paternalism (Tomlinson 1989)." (Mills, 2018), Meghan has stepped outside of these implicit norms and what is implicitly comfortable. As a counsellor, we listen out for the implicit voice, in communications. With your headline of: "Meghan and Harry haven't been criticised because of her color but because she's a selfish social climber and he's a weak whiner - and by playing this despicable race card they have grossly libeled all of Britain" (Mail, 2020), the implicit voice I hear, is 'How dare you'. Indeed, as I read more of your article, some of the lines begin with 'How dare....'"

In addition to the above implicit dynamics, there have also been the explicit headlines and comments.

"Harry's girl is (almost) straight outta Compton: Gang scarred home of her mother revealed – so will he be dropping by for tea?" (Mail, 2016)

"Now that's upwardly mobile! How in 150 years, Meghan Markle's family went from cotton slaves to royalty via freedom in the U.S. Civil War ... while her dad's ancestors included a maid at Windsor Castle." (Mail, 2017)

"MUM'S SIDE: DIRT POOR IN DEEP SOUTH." (Mail, 2017)

"Yes, they're joyfully in love. So why do I have a niggling worry about his engagement picture?" (Vine, 2017)

Markle could help add "rich and exotic DNA" to the royal family. (Mail, 2016)

"Miss Markle's mother is a dreadlocked African-American lady from the wrong side of the tracks." (Mail, 2016)

"Harry's girl on Pornhub." (Sun, 2016)

"MEET THE IN-LAWS: The VERY un-royal Markle family now set to liven up Windsor family Christmases." (Sun, 2017)

"NOT A DUPLI-KATE." (Sun, 2017)

"Seven reasons why Meghan Markle is nothing like Kate Middleton... from relationship history to fashion sense." (Sun, 2017)

Moving Forward

My sister recently said, when talking about the Global Black Lives Matter movement, that she felt there was no real leader, that we did not have a Martin Luther King or a Nelson Mandela of today. I agree, but perhaps think this might be something we can use to our advantage.

For instance, maybe it is time for us to work collectively to make a change and move forward together? Perhaps it is the time for each person to play their part.

Writing this book has been a journey. Doing the focus groups and interviews, reflecting on my counselling training and looking at research has been most insightful and confirmatory.

I was going to write here, my personal views for moving forward, but much of those thoughts are contained within the framework of this book, mapping the journey from attachment to systemic operation.

At the completion of the book, there are protests today in America at the shooting of Jacob Blake, yet another African American man killed by police.

Maybe this is the time and opportunity for us all to do the work towards change collectively.

THIS BOOK

Thank you for reading this book! It has been a real pleasure to write.

They say there is a book in all of us! This book is the first I have written, and the words seemed to flow onto the page.

It has been very much a cathartic exercise, to explore more of the macro picture of systemic racism, and to try to communicate this in an accessible way.

Your feedback on your reading experience of this content would be most appreciated! I would value it if you could leave your honest review on Amazon, or your source of purchase.

Many thanks,

Suzann

BIBLIOGRAPHY

(ERCOMER), E. R. C. o. M. a. E. R., 2002. *Racism and Cultural Diversity in the Mass Media,* Vienna: European Monitoring Centre on Racism and Xenophobia, Vienna (EUMC).

Academy, C. &. P. T., 2018. *Level 4 Diploma in Therapeutic Counselling - Integrative CPTA Course Handbook Sept 2018 to July 2020.* Lonfon: CPTA.

ADL, 2020. *Movies and the Diversity Gap (Incorporating Lee and Low Books Statistics).* [Online]
Available at: https://www.adl.org/education/resources/tools-and-strategies/table-talk/movies-diversity-gap
[Accessed 29 July 2020].

Akala, 2018. The great British contradiction. *RSA Journal,* Issue 2.

Akala, J. O., 2018. *Akala deconstructs race, class, and Britain's modern myths | Unfiltered with James O'Brien.* London: JOE.

Allnock, D. a. M. P., 2013. *No one noticed, no one heard: a study of disclosures of childhood abuse,* NSPCC: London.

Ann Blake, L. G. S. T., 2001. *England Through Colonial Eyes in Twentieth-Century Fiction.* Melbourne: Palgrave MacMillan.

Anon., 2019. Posttraumatic Slave Syndrome, the Patriarchal Nuclear Family Structure, and African American Male–Female Relationships. *Social Work,* 64(2), pp. 139-145.

Arnold E, Opoku K, 2020. *Information Sheet: Impact of Immigra-*

tion. London: Arnold E, Opoku K.

Association, A. A., 1998. *AAA Statement on Race.* [Online]
Available at: https://www.americananthro.org/Connect-
WithAAA/Content.aspx?ItemNumber=2583#:~:text=Evi-
dence%20from%20the%20analysis%20of,within%20so
%2Dcalled%20racial%20groups.&text=The%20continued
%20sharing%20of%20genetic,humankind%20as%20a
%20single%20species.
[Accessed 28 July 2020].

Banton, M., 1977. *The idea of race.* New York: Westview Press.

BBC, 2019. *UK 'has particularly extreme form of capitalism'.* [On-
line]
Available at: https://www.bbc.co.uk/news/business-50562518
[Accessed 8 July 2020].

BBC, 2020. *Racial gaslighting made me feel like a foreigner in my
own home - Tasnim Nazeer.* [Online]
Available   at: https://www.bbc.co.uk/bbcthree/ar-
ticle/904d9237-1b8a-49bd-a801-448942b8cb52
[Accessed 22 July 2020].

Becoming. 2020. [Film] Directed by Nadia Hallgren. s.l.: Netflix.

Bell, C. C. D. E., 2013. *Racism and Pathological Bias as a Co-Oc-
curring Problem in Diagnosis and Assessment.* Stroud: Newgen UK
Publishing LTD.

Benefits, M., 2020. *PTSD and Veteran's Symptoms.* [Online]
Available at: https://militarybenefits.info/ptsd-and-veterans-
symptoms/
[Accessed 27 July 2020].

Berne, E., 1964. *Games People Play: The Psychology of Human Relationships.* New York: Penguin books.

Bhopal, V. L. a. R., n.d. *Ethnicity, socio-economic status and health
research: Insights from and implications of Charles Tilly's the-*

ory of Durable Inequality, s.l.: Institute for Health and Society, Université Catholique de Louvain; Alexander Bruce and John Usher Professor of Public Health, Centre for Population Health Sciences, Section of Public Health Sciences, University of Edinburgh, Medical School.

Bowlby, J., 1973. *Separation: Anxiety and anger: Attachment and Loss.* London: The Hogarth Press.

Brown, B., 2011. *The power of vulnerability | Brené Brown.* Houston: TEDx Houston.

C.M. Steel, S. A., 1964. Contending with group image: the psychology of stereotype and social identity threat. *Advances in experimental social psychology,* Volume 34, pp. 379-440.

C.R. Snyder, S. J. L., 2006. *Positive Psychology: The Scientific and Practical Explorations of Human Strengths.* s.l.:SAGE Publication.

Charles Dickens, W. H. A. A. S., 1853. *Bentley's Miscellany, Volume 34, Slavery in New England.* London: Richard Bentley.

Chekroud, A. E. J. A. B. &. H. M., 2014. A review of neuroimaging studies of race-related prejudice: does amygdala response reflect threat?. *Frontiers in Human Neuroscience,* Volume 8, p. 179.

Clark McKown, R. S. W., 2003. The Development and Consequences of Stereotype Consciousness in Middle Childhood. *Child Development,* 74(2), pp. 498-515.

Corbin, C. M., 2017. Terrorists Are Always Muslim but Never White: At the Intersection of Critical Race Theory and Propaganda. *Fordham Law Review,* 86(2), pp. 455-485.

Crosswalk.com, 2020. *4 Important Things to Know about What Privilege Does NOT Mean.* [Online]
Available at: https://www.crosswalk.com/special-coverage/racism/important-things-to-know-about-what-privilege-does-not-mean.html
[Accessed 14 July 2020].

Danielle Thom, M. o. L., 2018. *Mapping the legacy of slavery in London's Docklands.* [Online]
Available at: https://www.museumoflondon.org.uk/discover/mapping-londons-legacy-slavery-docklands
[Accessed 4 August 2020].

Daron Acemoğlu, J. R., 2017. *The economic impact of colonialism.* [Online]
Available at: https://voxeu.org/article/economic-impact-colonialism
[Accessed 6 July 2020].

Davis, E. B. &. L., 1988. *The Courage to Heal: A Guide for Women Survivor's of Child Sexual Abuse.* New York: Harper & Row.

DiAngelo, R., 2019. *White Fragility: Why It's So Hard for White People to Talk About Racism.* s.l.:Penguin Random House UK.

Dictionary.com, 2019. *Imperialism.* [Online]
Available at: https://www.dictionary.com/browse/imperialism
[Accessed 21 July 2020].

Durham, A., 2020. *Adrian Durham@@talkSPORTDrive.* [Online]
Available at: https://twitter.com/talksportdrive?lang=en
[Accessed 15 July 2020].

Equality and Human Rights Commission, 2018. *Race report statistics.* [Online]
Available at: https://www.equalityhumanrights.com/en/race-report-statistics
[Accessed 29 July 2020].

Equiano, O., 1789. *The Interesting Narrative of the Life of Olaudah Equiano: or, Gustavus Vassa, the African.* London: s.n.

Erfani-Ghettani, R., 2018. *Racism, the Press and Black Deaths in Police Custody in the United Kingdom, Media, Crime and Racism, pp.255-275.* London: Palgrave MacMillan.

Everett, A., 1995-1996. The Other Pleasures: The Narrative Function of Race in the Cinema. *Film Criticism,* 20(12), pp. 26-38.

Faulkner, C. A. F. a. S. S., 2019. *Addictions Counseling: A Competency-Based Approach.* New York: Oxford University Press.

Fernández, B. P., 2009. *The Vanishing Cowboy and the Unfading Indian: Manhood, Iconized Masculinity and National Identiy in Larry McMurtry's Lonsome Dove and James Welch's Fools Crow and the Heartson of Charging Elk,* Barcelona: Universitat Autònoma de Barcelona.

Firman F, G. A., 1997. *Primal Wound: A Transpersonal View of Trauma, Addiction and Growth.* New York: State University of New York Press.

George J. Sefa Dei, L. L. K. a. N. K.-L., 2004. Playing the Race Card: Exposing White Power and Privilege (2004). *Counterpoints,* 244(Peter Lang AG), pp. 127-146.

Gilda, G., 2014. The Intergenerational Trauma of Slavery and its Aftermath. *The Journal of Psychohistory,* 41(3), pp. 181-197.

Gilda, G., 2014. The Intergenerational Trauma of Slavery and its Aftermath. *The Journal of Psychohistory,* 41(3), pp. 181 - 197.

Glancy, M., 2014. *Hollywood and the Americanization of Britain from the 1920s to the Present.* New York: I.B. Tauris & Co Ltd.

GMB, 2020. *GMB.* London: ITV Breakfast.

GOV.UK, 2020. *Face coverings: when to wear one and how to make your own.* [Online]
Available at: https://www.gov.uk/government/publications/face-coverings-when-to-wear-one-and-how-to-make-your-own/face-coverings-when-to-wear-one-and-how-to-make-your-own
[Accessed 30 July 2020].

Gregg, A., 2014. *Is "White Privilege" a Useful Concept in the Current*

UK Context?. [Online]
Available at: https://www.rota.org.uk/content/%E2%80%9C-white-privilege%E2%80%9D-useful-concept-current-uk-context
[Accessed 18 July 2020].

Gross, S. R., Possley, M. & Stephens, K., 2017. *Race and wrongful convictions in the United States,* Irvine: National Registry of Exonerations, Newkirk Center for Science and Society, U. of CA Irvine.

Guardian, T., 2018. *The NHS, Windrush and the debt we owe to immigration, Gary Younge.* [Online]
Available at: https://www.theguardian.com/commentisfree/2018/jun/22/honour-nhs-built-on-immigration-windrush
[Accessed 29 July 2020].

Guardian, T., 2020. *Belly Mujinga: police ask CPS to review rail worker's Covid-19 death.* [Online]
Available at: https://www.theguardian.com/law/2020/jun/05/belly-mujinga-police-ask-cps-to-review-rail-workers-covid-19-death
[Accessed 15 July 2020].

Guardian, T., 2020. *Labour accuses government of cover-up over BAME Covid-19 report.* [Online]
Available at: https://www.theguardian.com/politics/2020/jun/06/labour-accuses-government-of-cover-up-over-bame-covid-19-report
[Accessed 9 July 2020].

Guardian, T., 2020. *The Great British Battle: how the fight against coronavirus spread a new nationalism.* [Online]
Available at: https://www.theguardian.com/books/2020/may/16/the-great-british-battle-how-the-fight-against-coronavirus-spread-a-new-nationalism
[Accessed 29 July 2020].

Hall, P. C., 2013. *Britain and the Legacies of Slavery.* London: UCL, Minds Lunch Hour Lecture.

Hall, P. C., 2013. *Towards a New Past: the Legacies of British Slave-Ownership by.* London: UCL History.

HAMALAINEN, P., 2018. Reappraisal of: Crooked Lines of Relevance Europe and the People without History, by Eric R. Wolf. *Oxford University Press on behalf of the American Historical Association,* pp. 875-886.

Hennesey, P., 2004. *Blair calls for quota on immigrants from 'New Commonwealth'.* [Online]
Available at: https://www.telegraph.co.uk/news/uk-news/1463759/Blair-calls-for-quotas-on-immigrants-from-New-Commonwealth.html
[Accessed 10 July 2020].

Independent, 2006. *Who'd be a Traffic Warden.* [Online]
Available at: https://www.independent.co.uk/news/uk/home-news/whod-be-a-traffic-warden-5335333.html
[Accessed 15 July 2020].

Independent, 2020. *Andrew Banks jailed for urinating next to PC Keith Palmer's memorial.* [Online]
Available at: https://www.independent.co.uk/news/uk/crime/man-urinate-keith-palmer-memorial-andrew-banks-court-a9566301.html
[Accessed 29 August 2020].

Jennifer T Kubota, M. R. B. E. A. P., 2012. The neuroscience of race. *Nature Neuroscience,* 15(7).

Journalists, T. C. I. o., 2020. *Lusamba Katalay wept as he told how the loss of former BBC journalist Belly Mujinga, 47, from Covid-19 after she was spat at has destroyed the whole world for him and his 11-year-old daughter.* [Online]
Available at: http://cioj.org/lusamba-katalay-wept-as-he-told-how-the-loss-of-former-bbc-journalist-belly-mujinga-47-

from-covid-19-after-she-was-spat-at-has-destroyed-the-whole-world-for-him-and-his-11-year-old-daughter/ [Accessed 15 July 2020].

Justice, G., 2017. *Honest Accounts 2017: How the world profits from Africa's wealth*, s.l.: Global Justice.

Kendall, 2002. *UNDERSTANDING WHITE PRIVILEGE*. Albany: CPT.

Kendall, D. F. E., 2002. *Understanding White Privilege*, s.l.: Francis E. Kendall.

Kohnert, D., 2008. EU-African Economic Relations: Continuing Dominance, Traded for Aid?. *GIGA Research Programme: Transformation in the Process of Globalization*, Issue 82.

Kolk, B. v. d., 2014. *The Body Keeps the Score: Mind, Brain and Body in the Transformation of Trauma.* s.l.:Penguin Publishing Group.

Korn H. A., J. M. A. C. M. M., 2012. Neurolaw: differential brain activity for black and white faces predicts damage awards in hypothetical employment discrimination cases. *Social Neuroscience,* Volume 7, p. 398–409.

Kulaszewicz, K. E., 2015. *Racism and the Media: A Textual Analysis*, St. Paul, Minnesota: Sophia, the St. Catherine University.

Lammy, D., 2017. *The Lammy Review, An independent review into the treatment of, and outcomes for, Black, Asian and Minority Ethnic individuals in the Criminal Justice System*, London: David Lammy.

Lecture, U. M. L. H., 2013. *Britain and the Legacies of Slavery (11 June 2013).* [Online]
Available at: https://youtu.be/igr3ybicGP4
[Accessed 4 July 2020].

Litwack, L. F., 2009. *How Free Is Free?: The Long Death of Jim Crow (The Nathan I. Huggins Lectures).* 1st ed. Cambridge, Massachusettes: Harvard University Press.

LLP, B. &. A., 2018. *How to Heal Trauma By Understanding Your Attachment Style.* [Online]
Available at: https://brickelandassociates.com/understand-attachment-style-heal-trauma/#:~:text=Any%20style%20of%20attachment%20%E2%80%94%20other,emotions%20isn't%20built%20in.&text=Overwhelming%20distress%20is%20traumatic.,in%20attempts%20to%20manage%20emotions.
[Accessed 1 August 2020].

Mail, D., 2016. *EXCLUSIVE: Harry's girl is (almost) straight outta Compton: Gang-scarred home of her mother revealed - so will he be dropping by for tea?.* [Online]
Available at: https://www.dailymail.co.uk/news/article-3896180/Prince-Harry-s-girlfriend-actress-Meghan-Markles.html
[Accessed 22 July 2020].

Mail, D., 2016. *RACHEL JOHNSON: Sorry Harry, but your beautiful bolter has failed my Mum Test.* [Online]
Available at: https://www.dailymail.co.uk/debate/article-3909362/RACHEL-JOHNSON-Sorry-Harry-beautiful-bolter-failed-Mum-Test.html
[Accessed 22 July 2020].

Mail, D., 2017. *Now that's upwardly mobile! How in 150 years, Meghan Markle's family went from cotton slaves to royalty via freedom in the U.S. Civil War... while her dad's ancestors included a maid at Windsor Castle.* [Online]
Available at: https://www.dailymail.co.uk/femail/article-5130473/Meghan-Markles-upwardly-mobile-family.html
[Accessed 22 July 2020].

Mail, D., 2017. *Now that's upwardly mobile! How in 150 years, Meghan Markle's family went from cotton slaves to royalty via freedom in the U.S. Civil War... while her dad's ancestors included a maid at Windsor Castle.* [Online]

Available at: https://www.dailymail.co.uk/femail/article-5130473/Meghan-Markles-upwardly-mobile-family.html
[Accessed 22 July 2020].

Mail, D., 2020. *Piers Morgan: Meghan and Harry haven't been criticized because of her color but because she's a selfish social climber and he's a weak whiner.* [Online]
Available at: https://www.dailymail.co.uk/news/article-7881661/PIERS-MORGAN-playing-despicable-race-card-Meghan-Harry-libeled-Britain.html
[Accessed 16 July 2020].

Mail, D., 2020. *Staggering 85% of new coronavirus infections in Blackburn 'are among South Asians' as council limits number of people allowed to visit other homes to avoid full Leicester-style lockdown after Covid-19 spike.* [Online]
Available at: https://www.dailymail.co.uk/news/article-8524675/85-new-coronavirus-infections-Blackburn-South-Asians-local-lockdown-looms.html
[Accessed 30 July 2020].

Marcello Solinas, C. C. N. T. R. E. R. a. M. J., 2008. Reversal of cocaine addiction by environmental enrichment. *PNAS, Proceedings of the National Academy of Sciences of the United States of American,* 104(44), p. 17145–17150.

Mate, D. G. M., 2015. *The Power of Addiction and the Addiction of Power: Gabor Maté at TEDxRio.* [Online]
Available at: https://youtu.be/66cYcSak6nE
[Accessed 3 August 2020].

MATERA, M., 2016. Cultures of Colonialism in the Metropole. Introduction: Metropolitan Cultures of Empire and the Long Moment of Decolonization. *Oxford University Press on behalf of the American Historical Association,* pp. 1434-1444.

McKenzie, A. C. &. K., 2002. Does racial discimination cause mental illness?. *Brtish Journal of Psychiatry,* Issue 180, pp.

475-477.

McKown C, W. R., 2003. The Development and Consequences of Stereotype Consciousness in Middle Childhood. *Society for Research in Child Development, Wiley* , Volume Child Development Vol. 74, pp. 498-515.

Meltzer, M., 1993. *Slavery: A World History.* Boston, Massachusetts: Da Capo Press.

Mills, C. W. &. C., 2018. The Psy-Security-Curriculum ensemble: British Values curriculum policy in English schools. *Journal of Education Policy.*

Monish Bhatia, S. P. W. T., 2018. *Media, Crime and Racism (Palgrave Studies in Crime, Media and Culture).* Cham, Switzerland: Palgrave MacMillan.

Morgan, P., 2020. *PIERS MORGAN: Thomas Markle's anguished text messages expose Meghan and Harry as a heartless pair who care more for complete strangers than their own family.* [Online]
Available at: https://www.dailymail.co.uk/news/article-7890609/PIERS-MORGAN-Thomas-Markles-anguished-texts-Meghan-Harry-heartless-pair.html
[Accessed 31 August 2020].

Nadal, E. &. K., 2019. *Challenging Definitions of Psychological Trauma: Connecting Racial Microaggressions and Traumatic Stress.* New York: John Jay College of Criminal Justice – City University of New York.

Nadal, K. L., 2014. A Guide to Responding to Microaggressions. *CUNY FORUM,* 2(1), pp. 17-76.

Nancy Moyer, M., 2019. *Amygdala Hijack: When Emotion Takes Over.* [Online]
Available at: https://www.healthline.com/health/stress/amygdala-hijack
[Accessed June 2020].

Naughton, K. T. a. M., 2006. Being White. *Transactional Analysis Journal,* 36(2), pp. 159-171.

News, G. M. D. D., 2020. *The part of.* [Online]
Available at: https://twitter.com/DJSemtex/status/1283037325858148354?s=09
[Accessed 16 July 2020].

NHS, 2013. *News analysis: Controversial mental health guide DSM-5.* [Online]
Available at: https://www.nhs.uk/news/mental-health/news-analysis-controversial-mental-health-guide-dsm-5/
[Accessed 25 July 2020].

Noah Uhrig, M. o. J., 2016. *Black, Asian and Minority Ethnic disproportionality in the Criminal Justice System in England and Wales,* s.l.: Ministry of Justice Analytical Services.

Noelle M. St. Vil, C. S. V. a. C. N. F., 2019. Posttraumatic Slave Syndrome, the Patriarchal Nuclear Family Structure, and African American Male–Female Relationships. *Social Work,* 64(2), pp. 139-145.

NZ, S., 2020. *Conflict and Your Brain aka The Amygdala Hijacking.* [Online]
Available at: https://sportnz.org.nz/assets/Uploads/attachments/managing-sport/officials-and-volunteers/Conflict-and-your-brain.pdf/
[Accessed 3 August 2020].

Parker, R. N., 2010. *Slavery in the white psyche : how contemporary white Americans remember and making meaning of slavery : a project based upon independent investigation" ,* Northampton, MA.: Smith College.

Paulson, A., 2018. *Elmina Castle.* [Online]
Available at: https://youtu.be/gQEz1MUTtLA
[Accessed 4 July 2020].

Pérez, N. M. C. &. E. O., 2016. Race and Nation: How Hierarchy

Shapes National Attachments. *Political Psychology,* 37(4), pp. 497-513.

Post, W., 2016. *The staggering numbers that prove Hollywood has a serious race problem.* [Online]
Available at: https://www.washingtonpost.com/news/the-switch/wp/2016/02/23/its-too-loud-and-other-reasons-oscar-voters-ignore-black-movies/
[Accessed 29 July 2020].

Post, W., 2019. *'It's unreal': Three Baltimore men exonerated after 36 years in prison.* [Online]
Available at: https://www.youtube.com/watch?v=6NoPikVr2Zc&feature=youtu.be
[Accessed 16 July 2020].

Psychology, S., 2019. *Defense Mechanisms.* [Online]
Available at: https://www.simplypsychology.org/defense-mechanisms.html
[Accessed 28 August 2020].

Psychology, S., 2020. *Maslow's Hierarchy of Needs.* [Online]
Available at: https://www.simplypsychology.org/maslow.html
[Accessed 1 August 2020].

race, O. S. U. K. I. f. t. s. o., 2015. *Implicit Bias.* [Online]
Available at: http://kirwaninstitute.osu.edu/research/understanding-implicit-bias/
[Accessed 22 July 2020].

Reisigl, R. W. a. M., 1999. Discourse and Racism: European Perspectives. *Annual Review of Anthropology,* Volume 28, pp. 175-199.

Robin DiAngelo & Ozlem Sensoy, 2017. *Is Everyone Really Equal?: An Introduction to Key Concepts in Social Justice Education.* 2nd ed. New York: Teachers College Press.

SAGE, 1992. Reviewed Work(s): Racism and the Press by TEUN

A. VAN DIJK: Language in the News: Discourse and Ideology in the Press by ROGER FOWLE. *Discourse & Society,* Volume 3, pp. 378-383.

Sanders, M. H. a. C., 1984. Film as a Medium to Study the Twentieth-Century Afro-American Experience. *The Journal of Negro Education,* 53(2), pp. 161-172.

Schaverien, J., 2015. *Boarding School Syndrome: The psychological trauma of the 'privileged' child.* London: Routledge.

Schwab, G., 2010. *Haunting Legacies: Violent Histories and Transgenerational Trauma.* New York: Columbia University Press.

SMEDLEY, A., 1999. "Race" and the Construction of Human Identity. *American Anthropologist,* 100(3), pp. 690-702.

Society, N. S., 2017. *Veil debate: Should the UK ban the veil?.* [Online]
Available at: https://www.secularism.org.uk/veil-debate-should-the-uk-ban-th.html
[Accessed 30 July 2020].

Society, U., 2012. *Durable inequality.* [Online]
Available at: https://understandingsociety.blogspot.com/2012/07/durable-inequality.html
[Accessed 22 July 2020].

SPARC, 2010. *Conflict and Your Brain aka "The Amygdala Hijacking".* s.l.:s.n.

Standard, E., 2016. *Reggie Yates: There are no other young black men like me on telly.* [Online]
Available at: https://www.standard.co.uk/showbiz/celebrity-news/reggie-yates-there-are-no-other-young-black-men-like-me-on-telly-a3357466.html
[Accessed 15 July 2020].

Standard, E., 2020. *Belly Mujinga: 'No evidence of spitting' before Victoria station worker died with coronavirus, police say.* [Online]

Available at: https://www.standard.co.uk/news/crime/belly-mujinga-death-no-evidence-spitting-a4455371.html [Accessed 15 July 2020].

Statista, 2020. *Global advertising spending from 2010 to 2019.* [Online]
Available at: https://www.statista.com/statistics/236943/global-advertising-spending/#:~:text=It%20is%20estimated%20that%20advertising,compared%20with%20the%20previous%20year. [Accessed 15 July 2020].

Sun, T., 2016. *Harry's girl on Pornhub.* s.l.:s.n.

Sun, T., 2017. *MEET THE IN-LAWS The VERY un-royal Markle family now set to liven up Windsor family Christmases.* [Online]
Available at: https://www.thesun.co.uk/news/5008385/prince-harry-meghan-markle-engagement-family-windsor/ [Accessed 22 July 2020].

Sun, T., 2017. *NOT A DUPLI-KATE Seven reasons why Meghan Markle is nothing like Kate Middleton... from relationship history to fashion sense.* [Online]
Available at: https://www.thesun.co.uk/fabulous/5010683/meghan-markle-kate-middleton-differences/ [Accessed 22 July 2020].

T Schmader, M. J. C. F., 2008. An integrated process model of stereotype threat effects on performance. *Psychological Reveiw,* 115(2), pp. 336-356.

Taylor, M., 2014. *Trauma Therapy and Clinical Practice: Neurosciences, gestalt and the body.* New York: Open University Press.

Telegraph, L., 2020. *Blackburn lockdown fears: 'Don't stigmatise Asian people over virus spike'.* [Online]
Available at: https://www.lancashiretelegraph.co.uk/news/18585068.blackburn-lockdown-fears-dont-stigmatise-asian-people-virus-spike/

[Accessed 30 July 2020].

The Matrix. 1999. [Film] Directed by Wachowski L Wachowski L. s.l.: s.n.

Theidon, K., 2020. *The Fletcher School: Intersectionality & COVID-19: A Discussion with Fletcher Faculty and Students.* [Online]
Available at: https://youtu.be/o3t087kNYxE
[Accessed 26 July 2020].

Thomas, L. K., 2014. *Attachment in African Caribbean Families.* s.l.:Routledge.

Today, U., 2008. *The Human Brain in Space: Euphoria and the "Overview Effect" Experienced by Astronauts.* [Online]
Available at: https://www.universetoday.com/14455/the-human-brain-in-space-euphoria-and-the-overview-effect-experienced-by-astronauts/
[Accessed 10 July 2020].

Topos Partnership, J. D. B. E. D. J., 2011. *Social Science Literature Review: Media Representations and Impact on the Lives of Black Men and Boys,* s.l.: The Opportunity Agenda.

Toye, R., 2011. *Churchill's Empire: The World that Made Him and the World He Made.* s.l.:MacMillan.

Upbility, 2020. *Mother-Child-Attachment.* [Online]
Available at: https://upbility.net/blogs/news/mother-child-attachment
[Accessed 29 June 2020].

Van-Der-Kolk, 2014. *The Body Keeps the Score: Mind, Brain and Body in the Transformation of Trauma.* s.l.:Penguin.

Vine, S., 2017. *Yes, they're joyfully in love. So why do I have a niggling worry about his engagement picture.* s.l.:Daily Mail.

Watch, B., 2015. *Vote UKIP: the English national party in British-nationalist clothes.* [Online]

Available at: https://britologywatch.wordpress.com/category/british-nationalism/
[Accessed 29 July 2020].

Wikipedia, 2010. *Exoneration.* [Online]
Available at: https://en.wikipedia.org/wiki/Exoneration
[Accessed 26 July 2020].

Wikipedia, t. f. e., n.d. *Elizabeth Freeman.* [Online]
Available at: https://en.wikipedia.org/wiki/Elizabeth_Freeman

Winnicott, D., 2018. *The Maturational Processes and the Facilitating Environment: Studies in the Theory of Emotional Development.* New York: Routledge.

World, T., 2018. *Meghan Markle headlines in UK tabloids a lesson in British racism.* [Online]
Available at: https://www.trtworld.com/europe/meghan-markle-headlines-in-uk-tabloids-a-lesson-in-british-racism-17669
[Accessed 5 August 2020].

Zevallos, D. Z., 2015. *Dehumanisation, Superhumanisation and Racism.* [Online]
Available at: https://othersociologist.com/2015/02/07/dehumanisation-superhumanisation-racism/
[Accessed 7 July 2020].